with the compliments of

Peter John Garrard

creative crafts

Pitman Periodicals Ltd
**41 PARKER STREET,
LONDON, W.C.2**

Registered office:
39 Parker Street
London WC2
Registered in England
No. 109908

An Introduction to Art and Craft

AN INTRODUCTION TO ART AND CRAFT

RITA GREER

Pitman Publishing

First published 1974

Sir Isaac Pitman and Sons Ltd
Pitman House, Parker Street, Kingsway, London WC2B 5PB
PO Box 46038, Banda Street, Nairobi, Kenya
Sir Isaac Pitman (Aust.) Pty Ltd
Pitman House, 158 Bouverie Street, Carlton, Victoria 3053, Australia
Pitman Publishing Corporation
6 East 43rd Street, New York, NY 10017, USA
Sir Isaac Pitman (Canada) Ltd
495 Wellington Street West, Toronto 135, Canada
The Copp Clark Publishing Company
517 Wellington Street West, Toronto 135, Canada

ISBN: 0 273 00220 1

Text set in 10/11 pt IBM Theme, printed by photolithography,
and bound in Great Britain at The Pitman Press, Bath
G. 359:13

Contents

Introduction

The instinctive urge to make things is present in *all* of us to a degree. To express these instincts through art and craft can offer a richer life in terms of personal fulfilment: whether we choose painting and drawing or cookery and flower arranging the same creative instinct is fulfilled.

This book is an attempt to explain the basic elements of art and craft. It is intended primarily for beginners and the non-professional artist or craftsman who wishes to spend his or her leisure hours creatively. It may also be of benefit to those who have already taken up a craft as a hobby and wish to have a more thorough and general background knowledge.

The text and illustrations explain matters in as clear and straightforward a manner as possible. The reader's attention is drawn in turn to each of the basic elements which may be present in expressions of art and craft. They are: colour and tone, texture, pattern and rhythm, shape and form, style and function, size and proportion, illusion and perception. In a more practical vein, matters such as basic sketching, drawing and associated materials, presentation and composition, are discussed. An attempt is made to explain the creative process and to define the roles of artists and craftsmen in society. The book ends with exercises based on its contents, which may be useful as a stepping stone towards taking a more practical interest in a particular form of art or craft.

1 Colour and tone

One of the most important elements of art is *colour*. Everything in our world has a colour and we often use it to identify and distinguish one thing from another.

To see colour we need *light*. Light (daylight) is composed of all colours. If these are separated we see what is known as the *visible spectrum*. This occurs in nature when a rainbow forms and the sun's rays are broken up by raindrops. These seven visible colours are red, orange, yellow, green, blue, purple and violet. They are called *hues*, or *pure colour*. As well as these seven visible colours, there are two others we know of which are invisible to the naked eye: ultra-violet and infra-red.

It is the effect of light on surfaces which enables us to see colour. A surface *absorbs* some of the spectrum colours and *reflects* others. It is the colour, or colours, reflected that determine the colour of the surface. Black absorbs most spectrum colours, and reflects very little. White does the opposite, and reflects all the colours. (In rare cases people may be colour-blind to a particular section of the spectrum, which makes them incapable of identifying certain colours.)

To indicate some kind of visual order for those concerned with the application of colour, the spectrum is interpreted in a number of graphic ways, usually in the form of a circle or wheel.

If you experiment with mixing colour pigments you will find that you can make an endless variety of colours from only three — red, blue and yellow. These three, which cannot themselves be made by mixing other colours, are known as the *primary colours*. On the chart used in this book they are shown as circles.

Two primary colours mixed together will give you a *secondary colour*: red + yellow = orange, yellow + blue = green, blue + red = violet. These are shown on the chart as triangular shapes, between the primary colours needed to mix them.

If you mix a primary (round) and a secondary (triangular) this will make a tertiary. The resulting six colours are shown on the chart as squares.

Notice that all the colours on the chart are in their natural state, i.e. no white or black has been added to give *tints* and *shades*.

A *tint* is a hue (colour in its natural form) with *white* added to make it *lighter* (for example, pink is a tint of red, cream is a tint of yellow).

A *shade* is a hue with a darker colour, or black, added to make it darker, for example brown is a shade of orange.

A note here about the use of black in colour mixing. Black is a combination of the three primaries. If you add it to a colour it tends to take away the personality of that colour and it 'dies'. It also has the effect of producing green if used to darken yellow. It is better to use one of the naturally dark colours, such as purple or mauve, to do this.

Frequently, popular names are given to tints and shades in an attempt to identify characteristics. Paint and textile manufacturers use these names to generate interest — which can lead to confusion. Here are a few of the more widely used ones.

Yellow and orange
Tints: lemon, cream, peach, camel, tangerine, coffee
Shades: chocolate, mustard, gold, ginger

Red
Tints: pink, rose
Shades: cerise, ruby, maroon

Blue and green
Tints: lime, turquoise
Shades: emerald, navy

Mauve and purple
Tints: lilac, lavender
Shades: blackberry, aubergine

In some cases colours are named with an added description, e.g. donkey brown, leaf green, brick red, sky blue, air-force blue. You can see how complicated and vague these terms are. A colour is much more easily identified by naming the spectrum colour, from which it is derived and stating whether it is a tint or a shade.

The following terms are used for colour.

Scheme: a combination of colours. There are several types of scheme. These are the most widely used.

Polychromatic (poly = many, chroma = colour). A scheme involving the use of many colours from all parts of the chart.

Monochromatic (mono = one). A scheme involving the use of one colour plus its tints and shades if needed. (A pencil drawing is said to be 'in monochrome'.)

Analogous (similar). A scheme involving the use of colours which lie next to each other on the chart, plus their tints and shades if needed, e.g. red, reddish-orange and orange.

Colours which give maximum visual effect when combined are called *complementary*. These are easy to identify as they lie directly opposite each other on the chart, e.g. blue and orange.

Primaries are always complementary to their opposite secondaries. Tertiaries are always complementary to their opposite tertiary, e.g. blue-green is complementary to reddish-orange.

All colours can be described as being either 'warm' or 'cool', depending on how much red or blue they contain. Pure red is the warmest colour and pure blue the coolest.

Yellow and mauve can be either warm or cool, depending on what kind of bias they have towards blue or red. Example: a lemon can be a cool colour, an egg yolk is usually a warm colour. You will see the chart is divided into three sections, the central section being the one in which colours can be either warm or cool.

It is an attribute of warm colours that they 'advance' and of cool colours that they 'recede'. Of course colours do not really advance or recede but they appear to do so. If you look at two identical shapes, one red and one blue, the red one will probably appear closer to you and also slightly larger than the blue.

Tone is often mistakenly used to mean *shade*. In fact every variation of colour has what is called a tone value. All hues, tints and shades are tones of colour. The word is correctly used to describe how light or dark a colour is, in relation to black and white. Example: yellow is light in tone, purple is dark in tone. The chart shows a scale for measuring tone, ranging from white through gradually darkening greys to black. These tones can be divided into three main groups: light, medium and dark.

Black-and-white television is seen in tone. Although someone may be wearing a yellow dress, on the screen it will appear as pale grey. (If you have difficulty in determining the tone of a colour try to imagine what it would be like on black-and-white television.)

2

COLOUR CHART

primary

secondary

tertiary

Colour

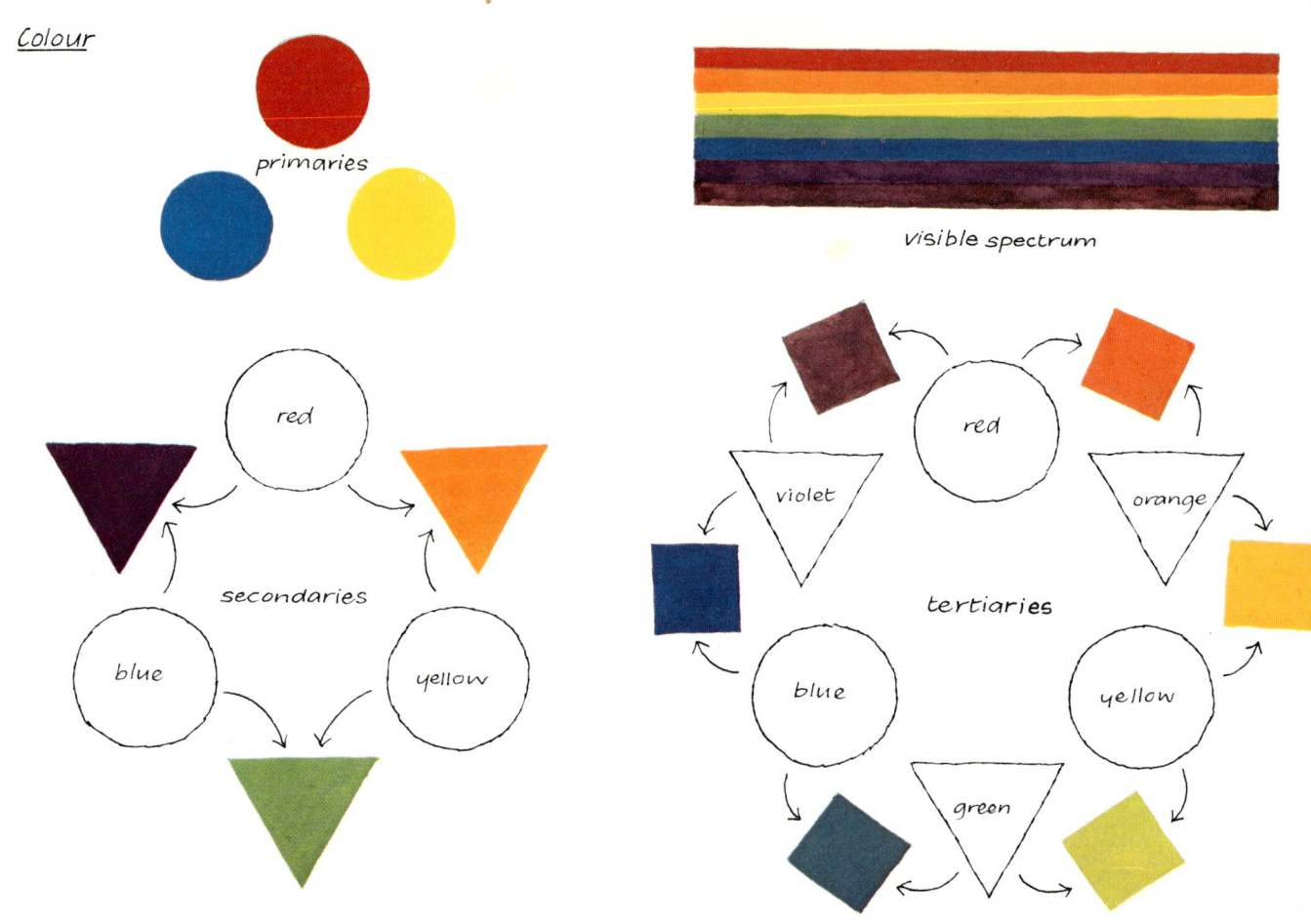

primaries

visible spectrum

secondaries

red
orange
yellow
green
blue
violet

tertiaries

red
orange
yellow
green
blue
violet

tints   shades   complementaries

hue   tints   hue   shades

SCHEMES

polychromatic   monochromatic   analogous

warm

warm
or
cool

cool

tone scale

natural tonal order

light

med.

dark

discords (reversed tonal order)

neutrals

colour influence

The natural tonal order of the seven hues (the spectrum) is: *light*, yellow and orange; *medium*, red, blue and green; *dark*, purple and violet. When the natural tonal order is upset, as when tints and shades are made, the colours produced can be very attractive and may give a more interesting effect if combined than would the colours from which they derive. For instance, brown (a shade of orange) and pink (a tint of red) are perhaps a more interesting combination than orange and red. Such combinations, which make use of reversed natural tonal orders, are called *discords*.

The widest range of colours that is still analogous consists of two secondary and four tertiary colours deriving from one primary (or, not more than one quarter section of the colour chart), and their tints and shades. An example would be red, orange and red-orange with pale orange, pink and brown. Each of these colours has a proportion of one basic colour, in this case red, to make them similar (analogous).

The narrowest analogous scheme would consist of the tints and shades of two adjacent colours.

Harmony and *contrast* are terms often used to describe the quality of colour relationships. 'Harmony' indicates a range of tones or colours which are very much alike in character, 'contrast' those that give an obvious contrast if combined. (Black and white produce maximum tonal contrast, complementary colours give a strong colour contrast.)

So far in this chapter mainly bright colours have been discussed — those with a high *chroma* or colour content. There is another category of colour with a low *chroma*, more usually called dull colour. The correct term is *neutral*, and it covers a large range of colours which have very little pure hue in them. It includes white, black and a large family of greys and near greys.

Colours can *influence* each other considerably when they are seen together. The illustration shows the same blue surrounded by red, yellow and violet. The influence of these surrounding colours slightly alters the character of the blue in each case.

The average person is aware of colour, but without the highly developed sense of the artist. We all tend to associate colour with certain emotions and events, based on our own experience and in folk-lore and myth. The following are some of the more obvious colour associations which illustrate this point.

Colour symbolism

Red fire, heat, passion, danger, action.
Blue calm, truth, infinity, sadness.
Yellow sunshine, joy, summer, warmth.
Orange mellowness, autumn, happiness.
Green coolness, freshness, serenity, growth.
Purple and violet wealth, nobility, mourning.
White purity, cleanliness, innocence.
Black tragedy, death, darkness, magic.

Everyone's colour sense develops according to his instincts and experience. Certain colours are more attractive than others to certain individuals, and most people have a favourite colour. Some are acutely aware of colour while others hardly seem to notice it. A wider understanding of the characteristics and value of colour can lead to a new awareness and sensitivity to the world around you.

2 Texture, pattern and rhythm

Every surface has a texture and texture plays an important
role in enabling us to distinguish between one object and
another. This is illustrated in the following drawings which
show a variety of surfaces, instantly recognisable by their
respective textures.

Textures

weaving   wood   fish scales   knitting

net   pebbles   fur   leaf

feathers   sea shell   hair   grass

The words used to describe texture can sometimes tell us how the texture came about (e.g. knitted, hammered, chopped), or from what material it is composed (e.g. woolly, silky). Often the tactile effect is of prime importance (e.g. scratchy, slippery). Some textures are even attributed with masculine or feminine characteristics. Smooth, fine and delicate textures such as silk, lace and satin suggest femininity, while coarse, rough textures such as bark, stone and rope are thought to be masculine. Other kinds of texture appeal to our emotions and can suggest such qualities as gentleness, harshness, etc.

When texture is described the scale generally used is: smooth, fine, medium, coarse, rough. Light and shadow enable us to see the elements of which a texture is composed, large elements usually producing a coarse texture and small ones a fine texture. We say a texture is *open* if the elements have plenty of space around them. A *close* texture is one in which the elements are grouped closely together with very little space around them.

While some textures appeal mainly to our sense of touch (e.g. fur, feathers and polished objects) another group will interest us visually (e.g. gemstones, ice-cubes). Others appeal to both sight and touch, especially in the case of food (e.g. potato crisps, pastry sprinkled with sugar or the crust of a loaf of bread).

Texture/space

open textures

close textures

6

Nature's textures are usually haphazard in the way in which elements are grouped —think of an area of turf, the pebbles on a beach. It is in the nature of man to make his textures orderly and regular, particularly where he has made the elements himself, as in a woven fabric, or a brick wall. This is probably because our minds prefer to organize texture into *pattern* where possible. Where this happens in nature, as it does in a honeycomb, crystal formations or ears of grain, we are usually impressed. Regular patterns are much easier to understand than haphazard ones. Which of the two arrangements, made from similar units, would you be able to remember?

Regular/haphazard arrangements

The following illustrations show a selection of basic repeat pattern arrangements (rhythmic repeats) used mainly for printed and woven fabrics and decorative surfaces.

Plain
2 × 2 threads

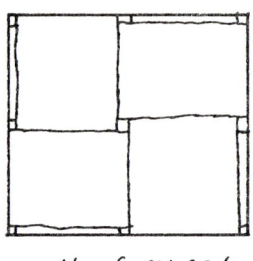

unit of repeat

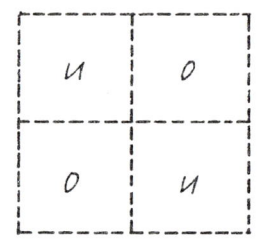

→ thread
(o = over, u = under)

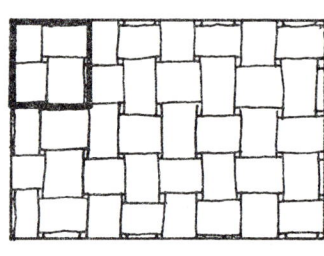

sample weave

Twill
4 × 4 threads

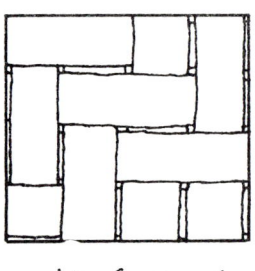

unit of repeat

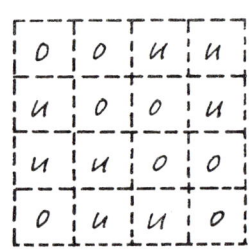

→ thread

sample weave

Basic weaving patterns/textures

Haircord
2 × 3 threads

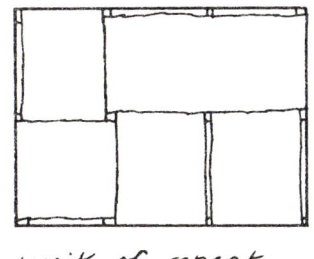

unit of repeat

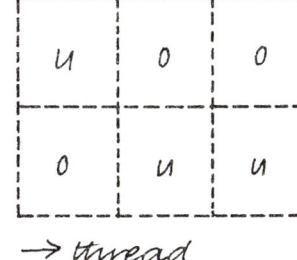

→ thread

sample weave

Herringbone
4 × 7 threads

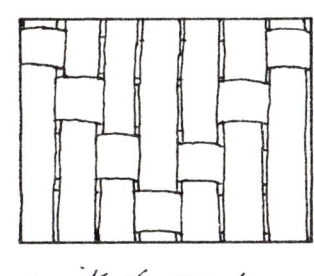

unit of repeat

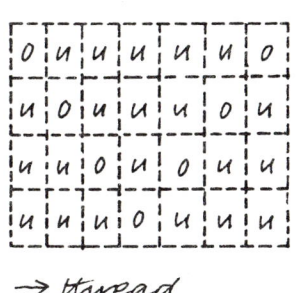

→ thread

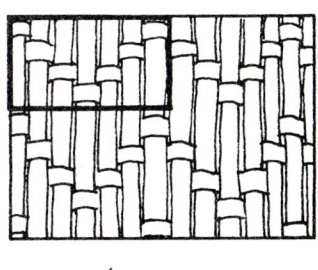

sample weave

9

Basic repeat patterns

Vertical stripe
Top and bottom
of units join
to make the
stripes continuous

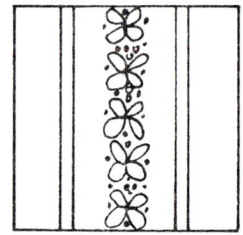

unit of repeat

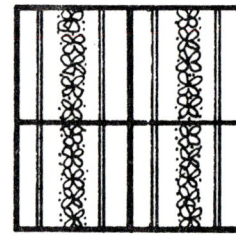

4 repeats

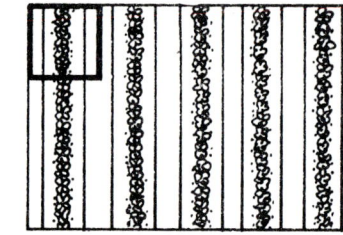

sample

Horizontal stripe
Sides of repeat
unit join up
to form stripes

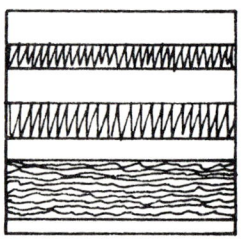

unit of repeat

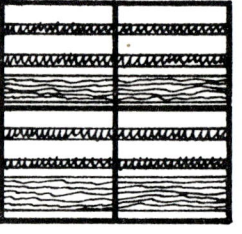

4 repeats

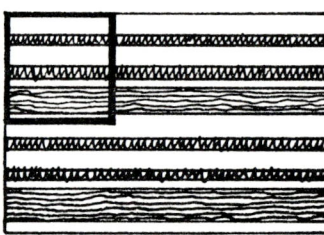

sample

Diagonal stripe

Repeats join top to bottom and side to side to give continuous stripes

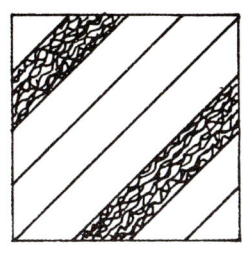

unit of repeat

4 repeats

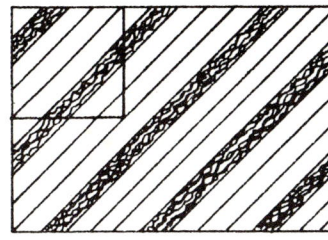

sample

Diamond repeat

Repeat divides into one central diamond and four triangles (4 diamonds)

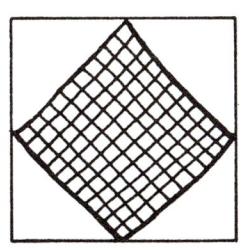

unit of repeat

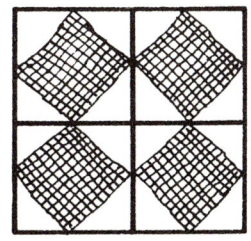

4 repeats

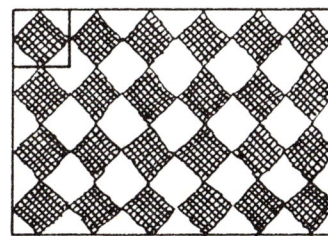

sample

<u>Spot</u>
Design is
isolated within
unit to form a
spot

unit of repeat

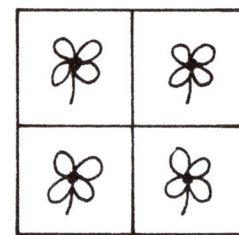

4 repeats

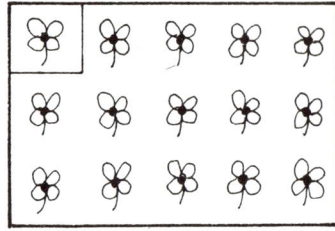

sample

<u>Counterchange</u>
Colours reverse
alternately. ↕ ↔
Four motifs make
unit of repeat.

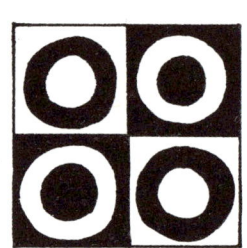

unit of repeat

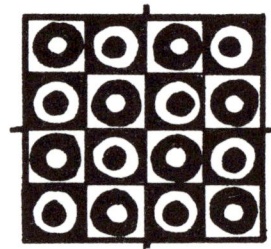

4 repeats

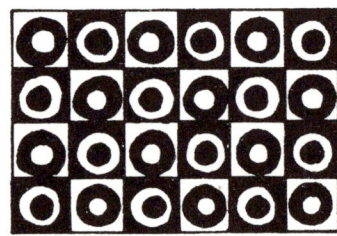

sample

Half-drop
Design drops
½ way down
once, within
the unit

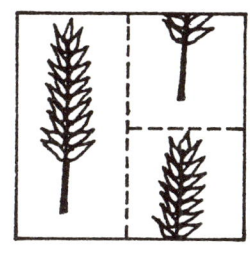

unit of repeat

4 repeats

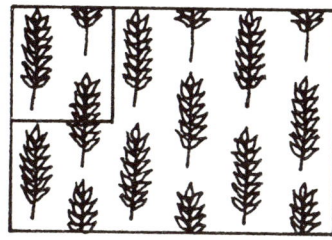

sample

Quarter-drop
Design drops
¼ way, ½ way,
¾ way down
the unit

unit of repeat

4 repeats

sample

13

Turning square

Motif in square turns regularly
($\uparrow \rightarrow \downarrow \leftarrow$) but gives
a random effect

unit of repeat

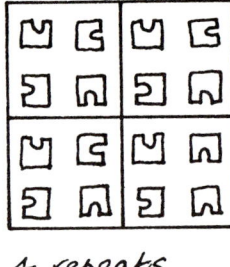

4 repeats

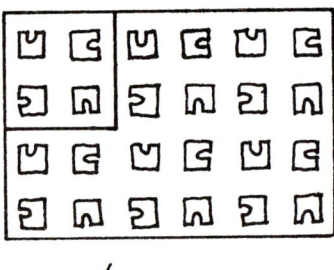

sample

Scattered

Various motifs
spread all over
unit. Joins at
top/bottom and
side/side.

unit of repeat

4 repeats

sample

14

The patterns, or rhythms, found in nature are more complicated than man-made ones and usually involve graduation in size of units. While not absolutely regular they appear to be so, similar shapes echoing if not repeating each other.

Rhythm

Shape

Variation in size and arrangement of similar units does not detract from rhythm of repeated shape of the seeds

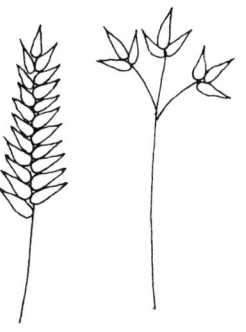

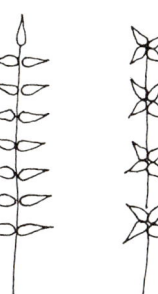

Generally speaking, rhythm occurs wherever repetition can be seen. It may be regular or irregular and can appear wherever one or more of the following kind of phenomena present themselves: colour, tone, size, shape, form, texture, line, direction, proportion, style.

Size

Repetition of a basic size of unit suggests rhythm even though the units vary in detail

3 Shape and form

Art uses the urge to form, or create, that is instinctive in man. Animals and birds also create — by building nests, burrowing, etc. — but there is no element of progress in their creativity. A sparrow today makes a nest in precisely the same way as a sparrow of a thousand years ago. It may make use of different materials but the *form* of the nest will not have changed at all. Man, however, combines his creative instincts with *ideas*. As his understanding and environment change so his ideas, and therefore his art, progress and take a new direction. The use and development of tools and machines as extensions and adaptations of the hands and feet have enabled us to increase our skills and open up new fields of exploration.

Artistic expression in shape and form communicates feeling and is part of the language of man's emotions. This is why we rely so heavily on our instincts when we try to judge the value of art. No two people will have precisely the same reaction to a work of art — a sculpture which appears beautiful to one person may well seem ugly to another.

Most people respond instantly to art forms by making noises rather than speaking. Something we find beautiful makes us gasp 'ooh' or 'aah'. If we find something which appears ugly we exclaim 'ugh'. This is a universal language of the emotions understood throughout the world. Along with the various noises go facial contortions and body movements. Many of us when confronted with a form we find repulsive will cover our eyes with our hands. Things we find beautiful can make us want to touch them and so increase our pleasure.

All these reactions point to very powerful instinctive emotions. Since everyone's emotions are individual there can

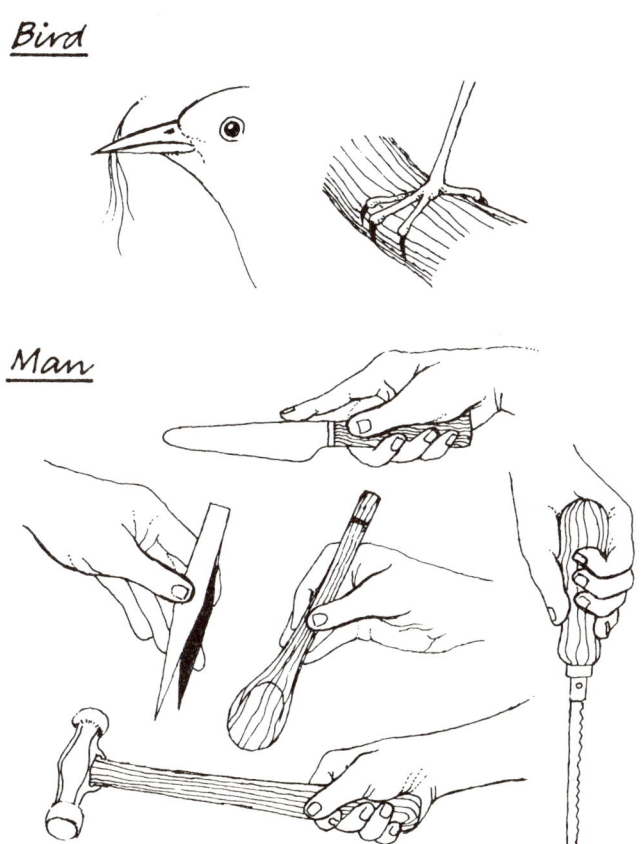

Bird

Man

17

be no universal measure for how good or bad art may be. However, every period in history has its own particular style in art which enables fashion and taste to direct and, to a great extent, assess it.

From a practical point of view shape and form are concerned with *dimensions.* Objects such as a chair or a table have three dimensions, *height, width* and *depth.* A drawing of a chair or table has only two dimensions, *height* and *width* but depth can be implied by using perspective and emphasis (see also Chapter 6).

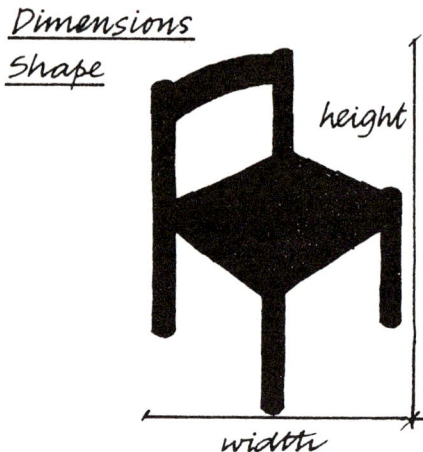

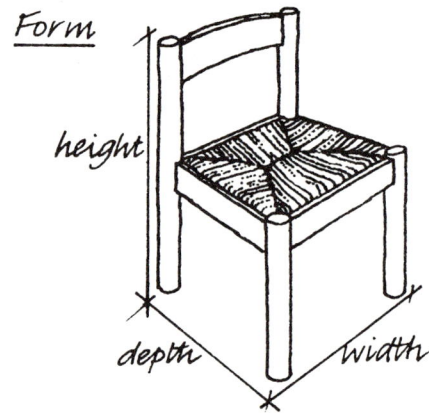

Three-dimensional forms are said to be 'in the round' (as is sculpture). Two-dimensional things are flat and concerned with shapes (as is a drawing of a head). Objects which are in between are called 'in relief' or 'bas-relief' (*bas* means low), for example the monarch's head on a flat coin.

The shapes and forms found in nature are usually very complex. They are *organic*, that is created by growth, and no two are identical, although they may be similar. Take the branch of a tree in summer and look at its leaves. They are basically all the same type, but each will vary slightly in shape, colour, weight, texture, length, width, age, etc.

We can draw shapes mechanically with various tools like rulers and compasses so that they can be repeated. Machines and moulds can provide a means of repeating three-dimensional forms (for instance, buckets and plastic bags). These are inorganic, that is, they are not created by natural growth.

Sculpture
Three-dimensional forms 'in the round'

Drawing
Concerned with two-dimensional shapes

Coin
Uses flattened forms on a flat background – 'bas relief'

Just as organic shapes and forms are complex, inorganic ones are generally simple, based on straight lines and regular curves. Even a complicated piece of machinery such as a clock is made up of reasonably simple, geometrically shaped parts.

The counterpart of a form is the *space* left around it. Sometimes this can be as important as the form itself. By moving the form about you may organize the space it leaves, as for example you might by moving the furniture about in a room. What we call 'planning' in interior design is largely the organization of space.

We learn very quickly to estimate the volumes of space and form because of their close relationship. When you are packing a parcel you automatically assess how much larger the box has to be than the object you are packing in it.

In a two-dimensional work, such as a drawing, the same sort of assessment must be made to estimate the *area* of a shape. The counterpart of that area is called the *negative shape* or *shape left*.

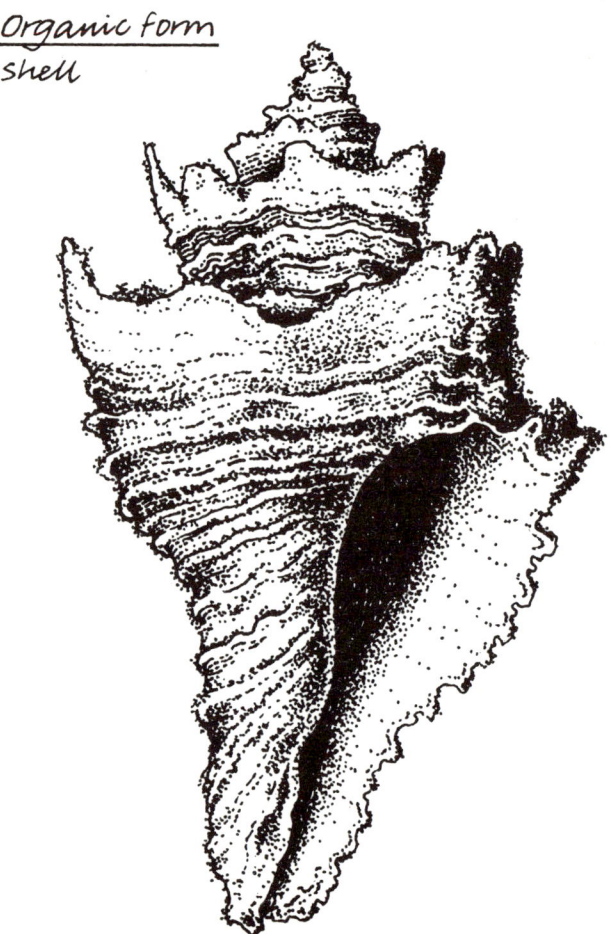

Organic form
shell

20

Inorganic shapes - clock parts

Drawn Shapes

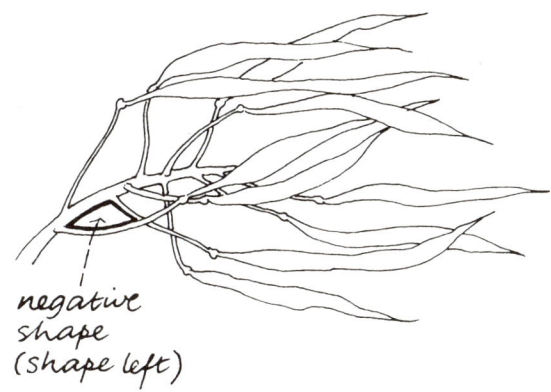

negative
shape
(shape left)

Just as texture can suggest definite psychological attributes, so can shapes and forms. Generally speaking shapes made from straight lines are 'stronger' than those made from curves. Forms which are actually heavy give a *feeling* of strength and weight while ones of little substance convey a feeling of lightness and grace.

The end product of any visual art process will comprise shapes and, or, forms. It is these that provide us with evidence of man's creativity and imagination, and also a record of social, economic and personal comment made at a specific point in time.

Heavy forms

Although curves are used in the design of this chair, its visual weight suggests strength

Straight lines and large forms combine to make a very strong, solid looking chair

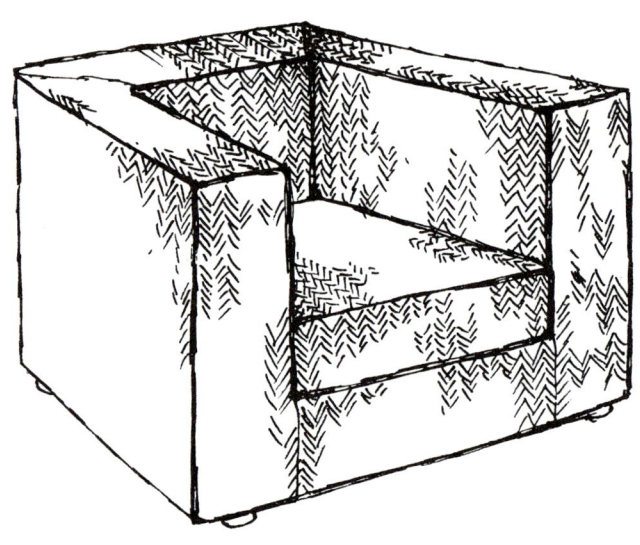

Light forms

A series of curves makes this light chair appear almost flimsy

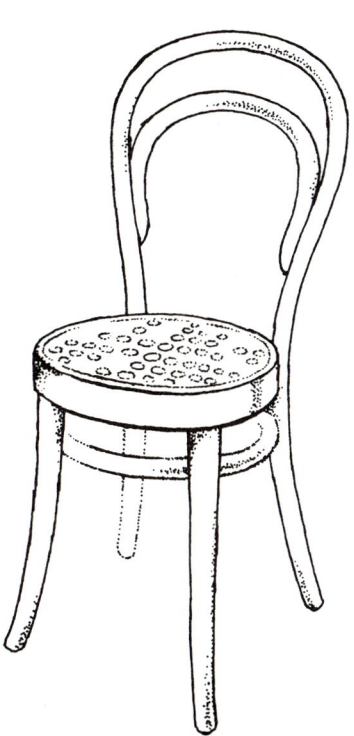

Although a light form, this chair looks strong because mainly straight lines have been used in its design

4 Style and function

Style is the manner in which something is made. In its widest
sense it is the way in which a particular culture expresses itself
through the art it produces. As a culture develops, and is sub-
jected to different pressures, so its style changes. This results
in a change of direction in art and the creation of a new
movement.

   In the more sophisticated cultures of the world objects can
easily be identified as belonging to a particular period in
history. The illustrations show how one object can vary in
style according to the time of its manufacture, in this case a
woman's dress.

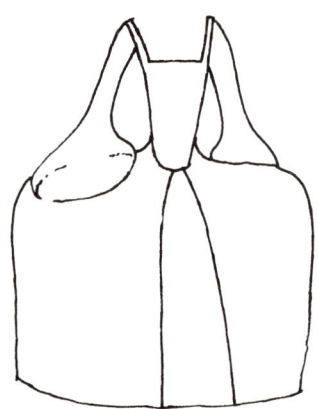

Style

Ten variations in the
basic style of a dress.
Each garment was made
during a different period
in history.

(17th – 19th century)

(19th – 20th century)

25

Looking at a variety of objects from the same period you will see how a certain *mood* or *feeling* prevails in all the forms, in spite of all the objects having totally different uses and being made by different artists. The examples show objects in the Art Nouveau style, a movement at its height in France around 1900. The main elements they have in common are their use of natural forms, particularly flowers, supple curves, the feeling of femininity and elegance, and a freshness of approach.

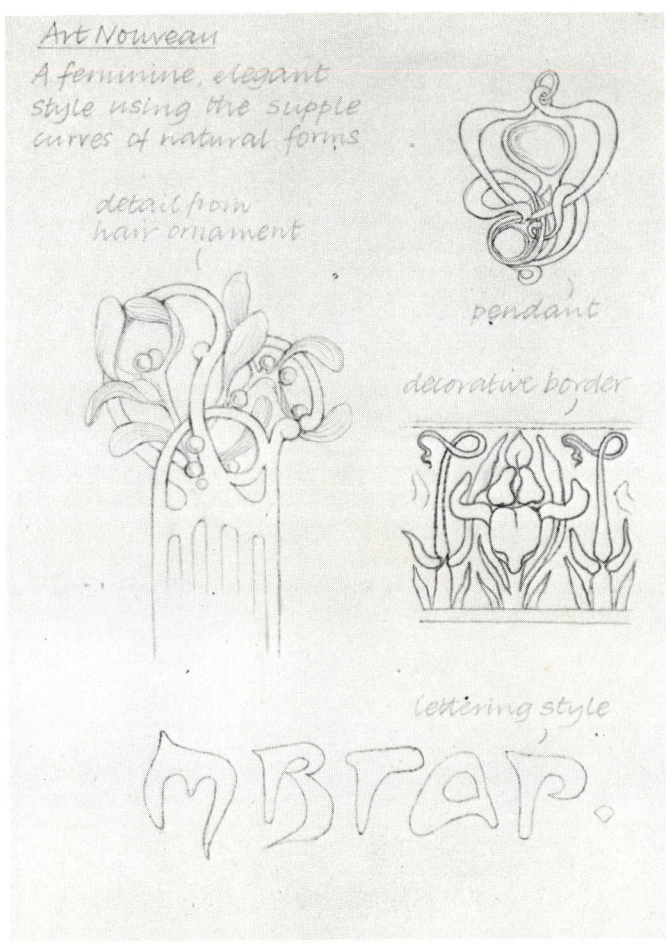

Art Nouveau

A feminine, elegant style using the supple curves of natural forms

detail from hair ornament

pendant

decorative border

lettering style

figure with flowers

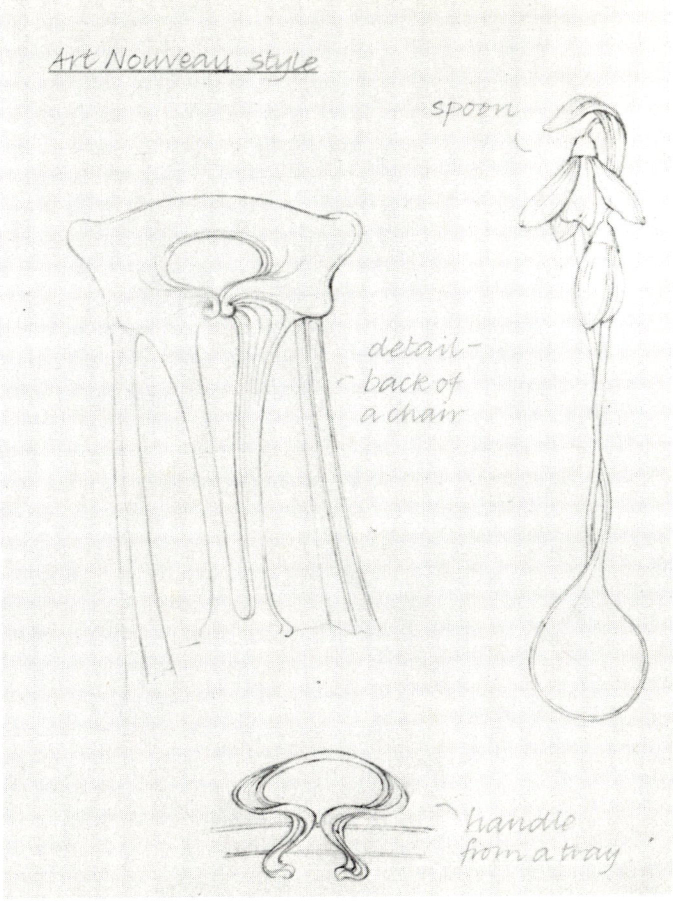

Art Nouveau style

spoon

detail –
back of
a chair

handle
from a tray

Like all movements in art, Art Nouveau was the result of a combination of many economic and social factors. In this case the most important influences were the interchange of cultural ideas with Japan, and great progress in industry, which produced many new technical inventions. Other factors were the emergence of several leaders who inspired the artists and craftsmen of the day, and their encouragement by an affluent society centred in Paris and supported by a huge increase in foreign trade.

Followers of the style in other countries were influenced by France but did not produce work of the same quality or feeling, as they were working in a different environment, and were therefore exposed to different influences. English followers produced work with religious overtones, and without the freshness and lightness of the French style.

Several movements, or styles, in art can develop simultaneously. This is because style cannot be forced on society; people have to be willing to accept and use it. Style is one way of expressing new ideas and not everyone is willing to accept change readily. The sketches show two domestic interiors of 1972, both using furniture and fittings which could be bought easily during that year. They illustrate the contrast in style of merchandize available.

Fashion is a concentration of style, often rather extreme and consequently of a temporary nature, which followers of fashion can copy and adapt to their own needs. The illustration shows how an exaggerated fashion in clothes is copied and adapted for mass production, and further adapted for widespread use as a paper pattern for the amateur. Note how the basic shape of the ensemble becomes less and less extreme.

28

Contrast in style

1972 interior (modern)

1972 interior (traditional) — same room

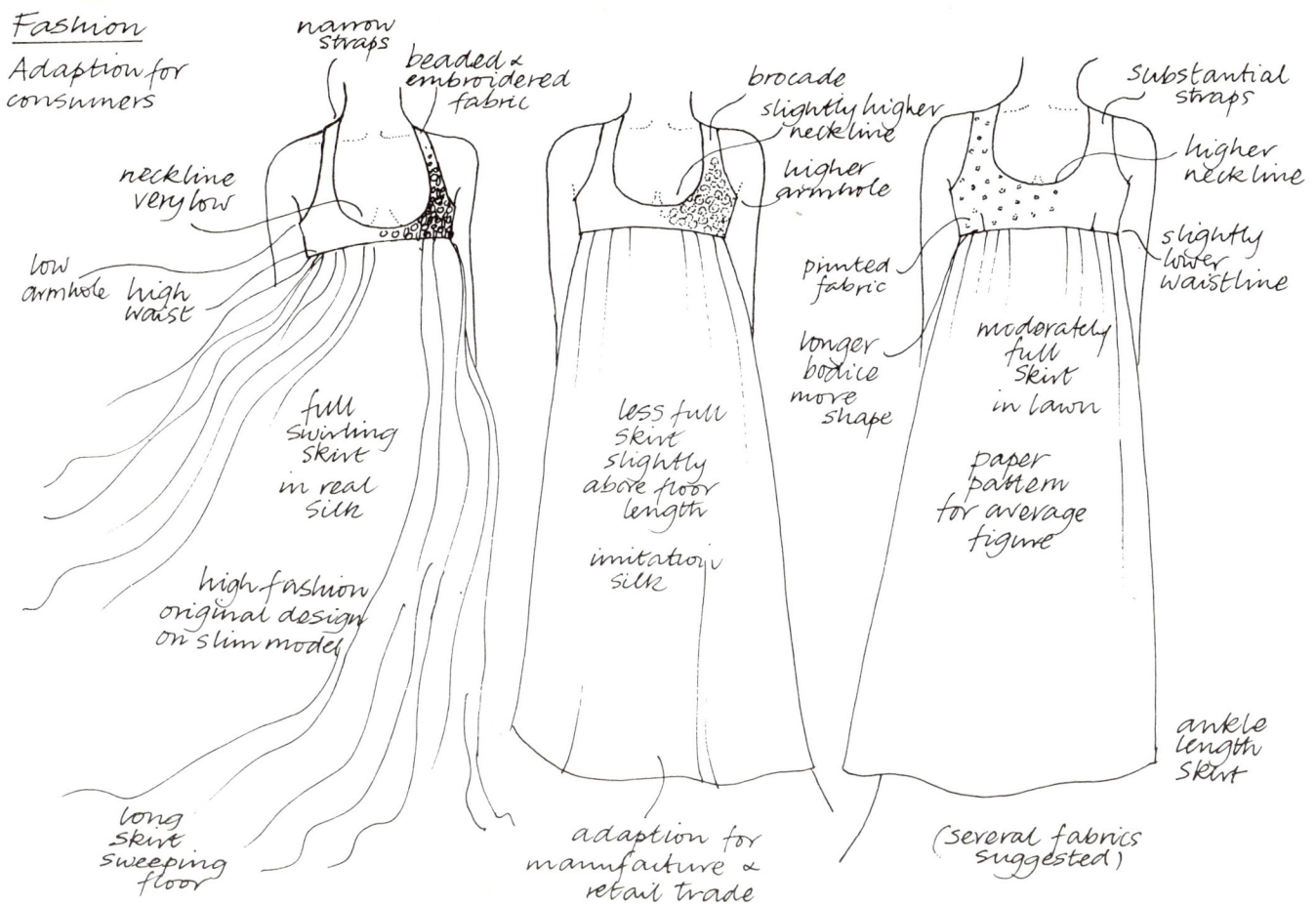

Fashion
Adaption for consumers

narrow straps

beaded & embroidered fabric

neckline very low

low armhole   high waist

full swirling skirt in real silk

high fashion original design on slim model

long skirt sweeping floor

brocade slightly higher neckline

higher armhole

less full skirt slightly above floor length

imitation silk

adaption for manufacture & retail trade

substantial straps

higher neckline

slightly lower waistline

printed fabric

longer bodice more shape

moderately full skirt in lawn

paper pattern for average figure

ankle length skirt

(several fabrics suggested)

Revivals of style occur from time to time, usually when there is social or economic instability, combined perhaps with a lack of emerging talent and leadership. Usually a revival of a style is a debasement of the original. The illustration shows one such example.

Some kinds of art change very slowly because the economic and social factors that control them undergo little change. Peasant art, where a style is passed by tradition from one generation to another, is an example.

There are two ways in which every individual helps to perpetuate a style. One is by choosing products conforming with that style (clothes, furniture, works of art). The other is by creating work in that style and adapting it to his own needs.

On a more personal level, everyone has his own particular style, or way of working, due very much to his personality. No two people can produce identical work even if one copies from the other. You have only to look at the variation between one person's handwriting and another's to see how much we are individuals.

The style of a useful object can be governed largely by its *function*. This is concerned with *purpose* and *activity*. To say something is 'functional' implies that it fulfils the purpose for which it was made.

Before designing or making a useful object several aspects of its function have to be considered. Taking the example of a spoon, these are basic factors which apply to most spoons, no matter what their specific purpose.

In general a spoon consists of a handle and a hollow end piece (bowl) for holding soft, liquid or fine-textured food. Depending on the use for which the spoon is intended the designer must consider such aspects as the size and shape of the bowl and handle, the material and method of manufacture.

Style

Real Tudor house – early 16th century

Mock Tudor house – early 20th century

He must also take into consideration the objectives involved in the actual use of the spoon. For example, the purpose of a coffee spoon is primarily to stir hot coffee. It may also be used for transferring sugar from a bowl to the coffee cup. It is used in conjunction with a coffee cup and saucer, and is held in the fingers. From this the designer understands that the bowl of the spoon must be sufficiently large and hollow to hold a portion of sugar but not too large to prevent the user from stirring inside the cup. The handle must be long enough to enable the user to hold it without getting his fingers in the coffee, but not too long to prevent it being laid in the saucer. It will need to be made of a material which can withstand the heat of the coffee.

These are merely the main considerations involved; there are also many minor ones important to the designer. Having made his observations concerning the factors which limit the size and shape of the spoon, he can then make a design working within the framework of his research. Note how important the relationship is between the spoon, the user and the cup and saucer: the spoon itself is part of a sequence of actions and objectives.

In general we are disappointed with objects that are merely functional and nothing more and at the same time those concerned only with style can make us frustrated. We are contemptuous of things made unskilfully yet skill for its own sake does not command our respect. To make something which is both functional *and* stylish is a difficult task. It requires a careful balance of the two: if one is sacrificed for the other the result is seldom satisfactory.

5 Size and proportion

If you saw an object, such as a cube, floating in space you would have no idea how large it was. To understand the size of an object you must be able to compare it with another object. In this way a comparison in sizes can be made and you can say, as in this case, A is larger than B.

To estimate the actual size of each of the cubes you would need to compare them with an object *whose size you already understand.* In this case the diagram shows the cubes on a chair, which immediately establishes their size. (A is about 6in cubed and B is about 3in cubed.)

Another example would be a vehicle travelling through space. Without a man for reference you would have no idea whether the spacecraft was 5 or 50 feet long.

As the sun sets and nears the horizon it looks larger to us than when it is overhead in the sky. In reality it is the same size but, as it sets, we can relate it to what is visible on the horizon – trees, buildings, etc. When it is high in the sky there is nothing with which to compare it. (We cannot use clouds as these vary in form and size.)

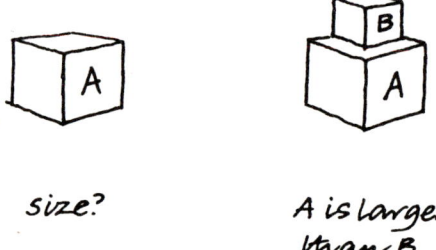

size?   A is larger than B

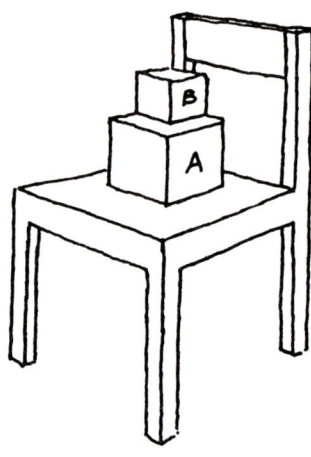

size established

32

Size/scale

size?

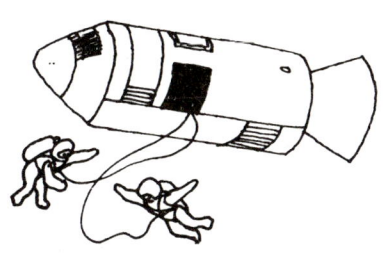

men establish scale

Size

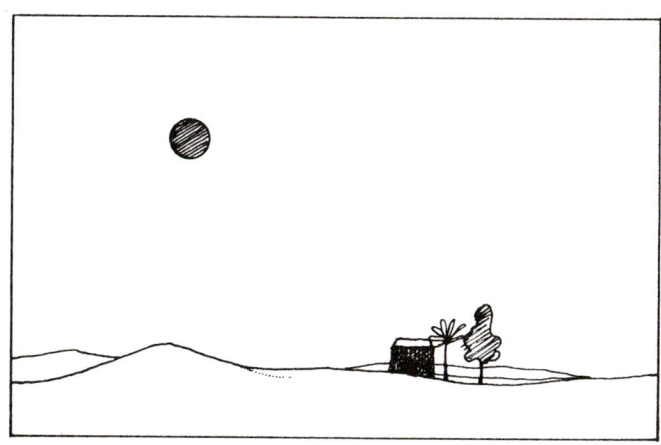

Sun is the same size in each sketch

From experience we learn to recognize which objects are liable to vary in size and which are not.

When possible we like to use a non-variable object for comparison. For example, to tell the size of a matchbox (variable) we automatically compare it with a match (non-variable).

Variable sizes

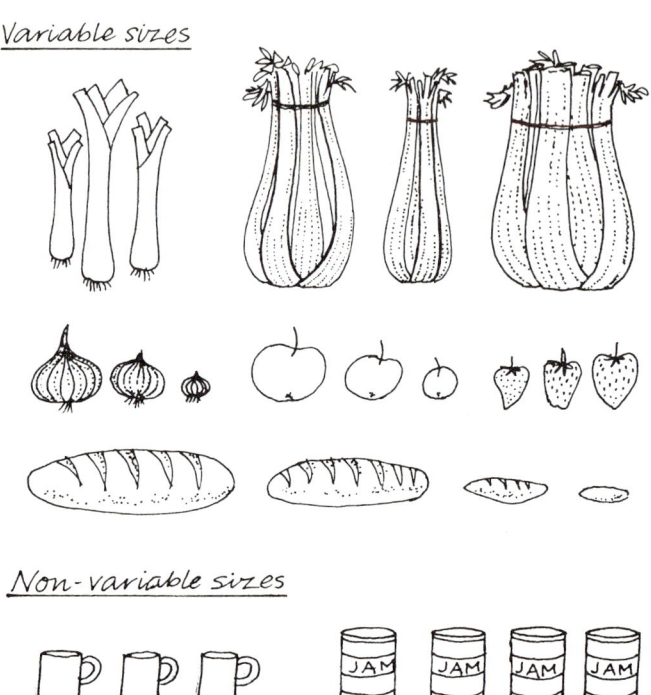

Size

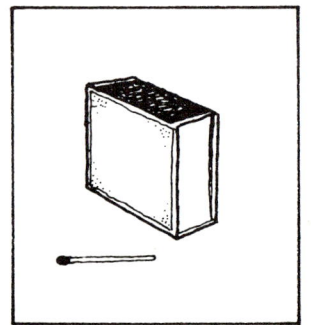

Match (non-variable) is used as a measure to determine size of boxes

Non-variable sizes

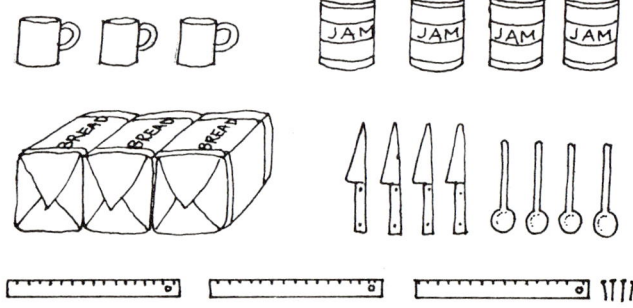

For objects likely to vary we get to know what size an *average* object of the same kind would be.

This gives a vague, as opposed to precise, scale of measurement which everyone more or less understands. For precise measurement man has invented several scales which are now used universally (e.g. the metric system for length, weight, temperature, etc.).

We very often use our own bodies as a kind of ruler. 'It was as long as my arm.' 'The grass is waist high.' 'It was no bigger than my thumb.' In particular we like to use our height as a measure and sometimes we relate our own bulk to forms.

For the objects man uses the average size of a person supplies the scale, but some with specialized uses are scaled up or down. The illustration shows a child's chair.

<u>Size</u>
Chair scaled down for child

Proportion means the relationship of one thing to another. It is a term used mainly for comparisons contained within one object. A proportion of something means a part of it (One of the difficulties in drawing is getting the proportions right. Common mistakes are underestimating the size of hands and feet and overestimating the size of the head.)

As when assessing size, to calculate proportion you need to compare one measurement with another. The drawing of the table in two dimensions shows that:

b = twice the length of a
d = 1½ times the length of a
$a = c$

These are the kind of comparisons that have to be made in drawing. The need to understand proportion also occurs when you are concerned with materials, for instance when mixing paint. (To make pink you need a *large proportion* of white and a *small proportion* of red: experience will teach you to judge the proportions that will give you the colour you want.)

Every human body has its own built-in measurements of proportion. One part relates directly to another making a kind of harmony.

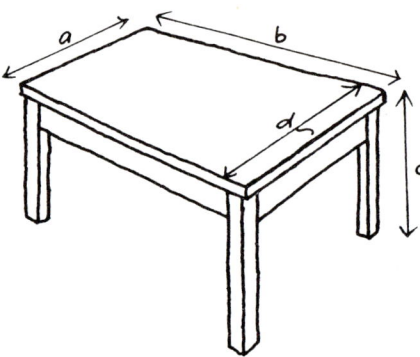

Comparisons
Length of line

36

Natural harmony

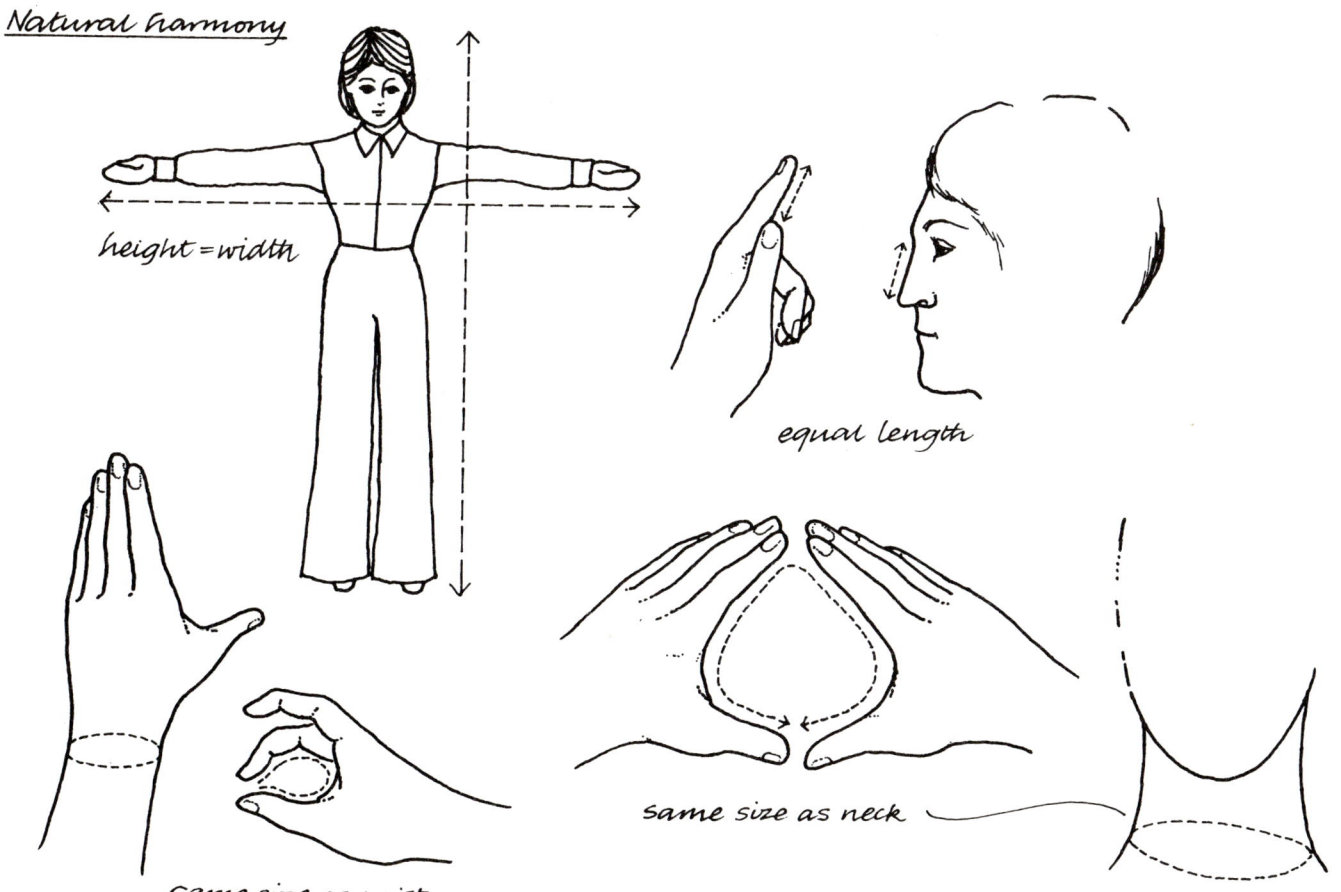

height = width

equal length

same size as wrist

same size as neck

Man has tried for many centuries to translate this kind of harmony which occurs in nature into a geometrical law. The Greeks arrived at what is called the Golden Section, or Golden Mean, and used it in their art and architecture. The recognized approximate formula for this is a series of measured proportions in which three bears the same relationship to five as five does to eight (3:5:8). The theory put into practice produces very satisfying and beautiful proportions, as can be seen in Greek art. It can also be applied to all natural growing forms (e.g. any fully-grown plant). The illustration shows it related to a portion of a stem with a leaf. Notice how the size of the units varies but the scale of proportion does not; it is always 3:5:8.

Your own body probably conforms to the Golden Section. If the body is divided into eight equal units the navel usually occurs at the 3/5 unit level as shown.

Man-made objects are often based on the Golden Section.

So far only measurements of length have been used. The formula can also be applied to area.

Over the centuries various rules for achieving good proportion have been devised, but that of the Golden Mean is the most satisfactory. However, although it can be a useful device it must not be thought of as the be-all and end-all of the creative process.

You will have seen how the assessing of size and proportion requires us to make *measurements* and *comparisons*. This is one of the most important aspects of drawing and one which although instinctive for some others have to toil at.

Dividing a line by the Golden Section

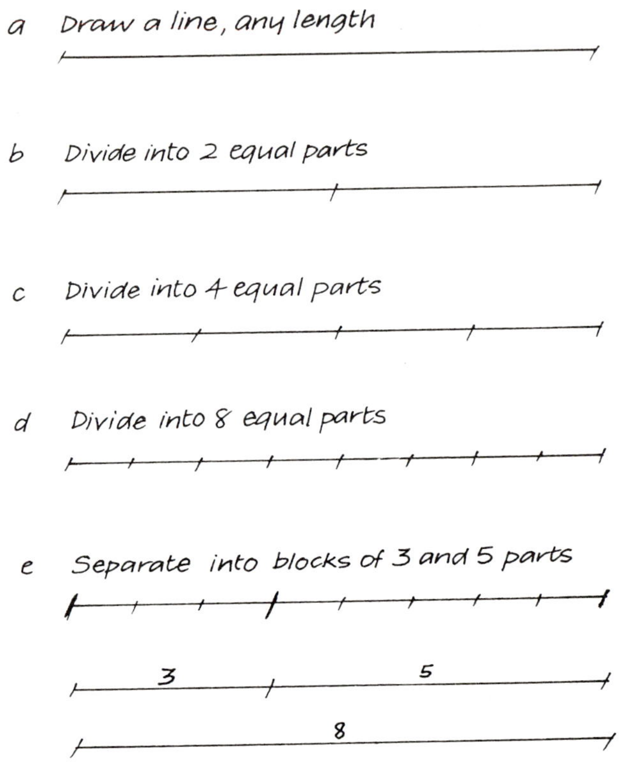

a   Draw a line, any length

b   Divide into 2 equal parts

c   Divide into 4 equal parts

d   Divide into 8 equal parts

e   Separate into blocks of 3 and 5 parts

3

5

8

The Golden Section, applied to an organic form — portion of a stem with seedpods

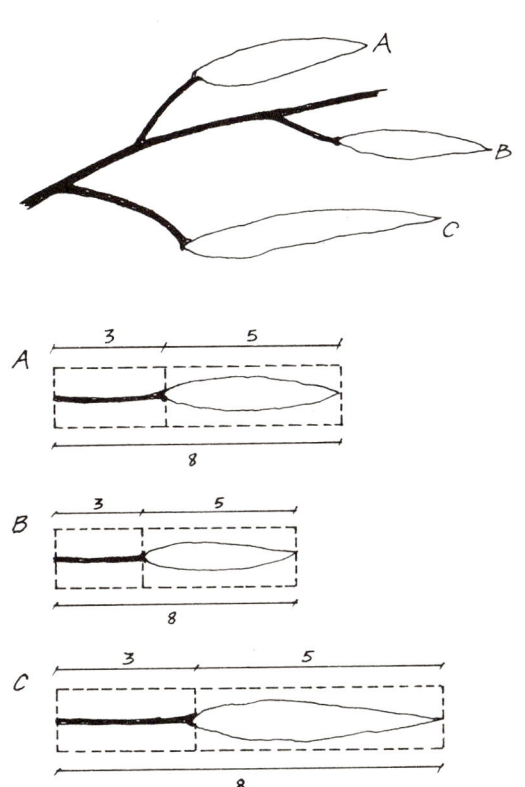

The Golden Section — related to the human body

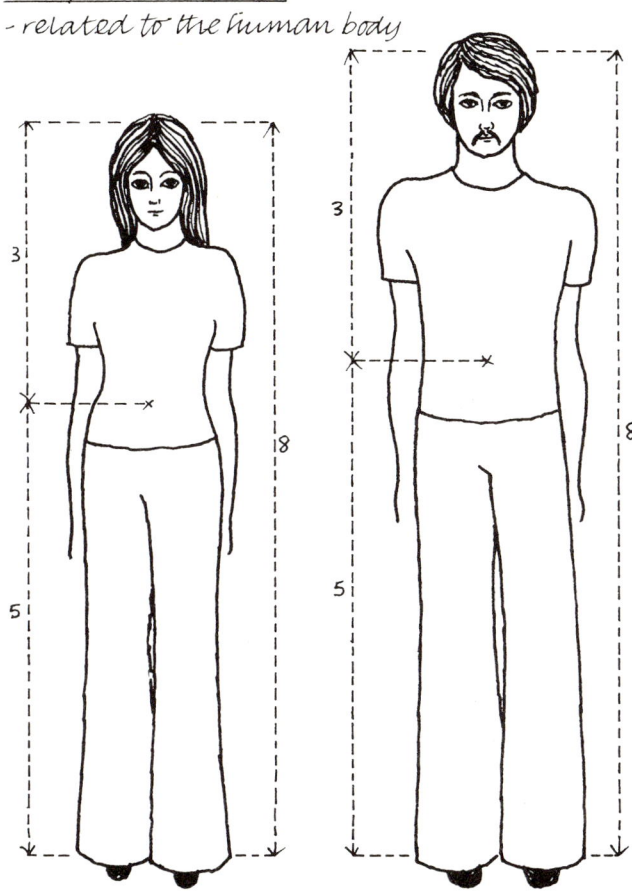

39

Man-made objects based on
Golden Section proportions

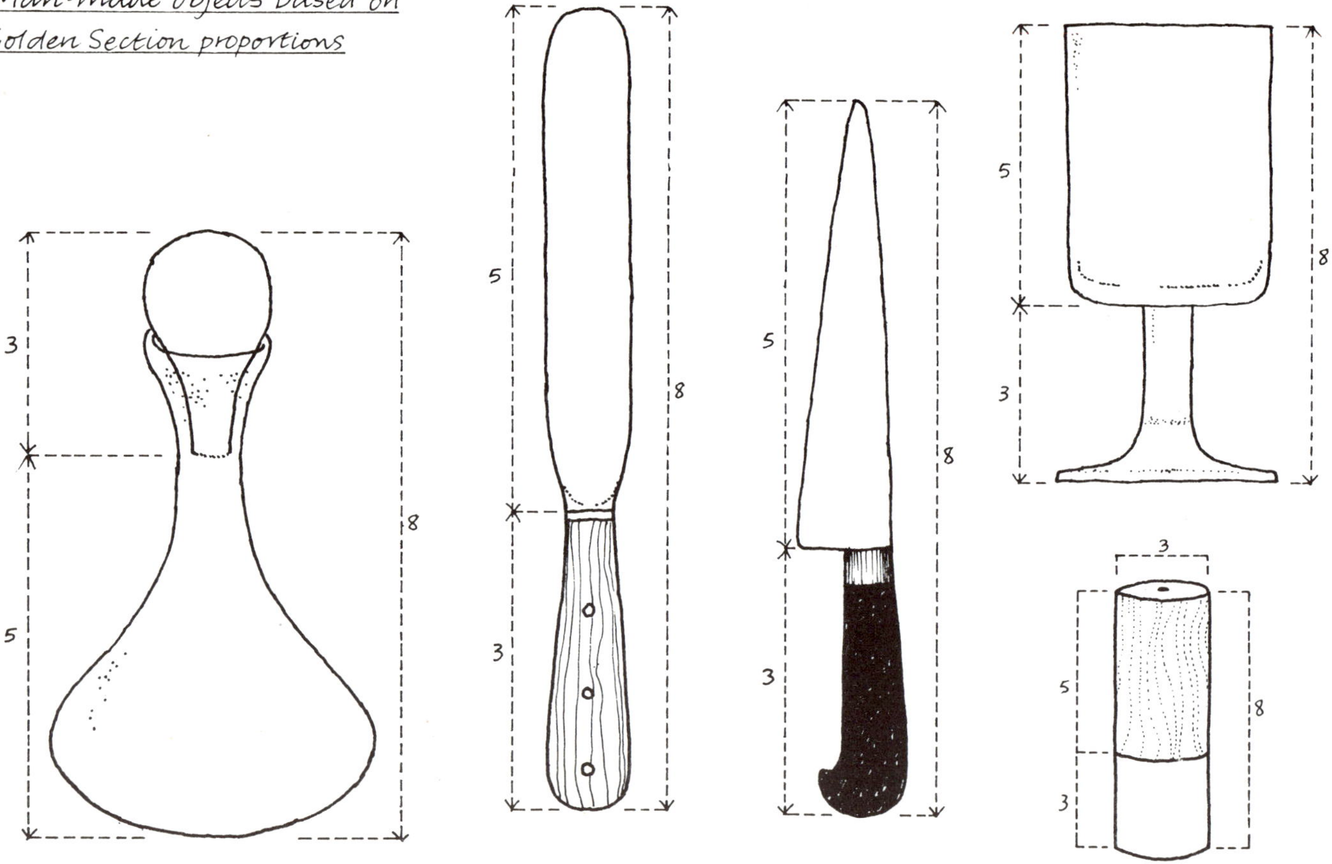

3
5
8

5
3
8

5
3
8

5
3
8

3
5
3
8

<u>The Golden Section proportions</u> — each whole rectangle (8 parts) is divided into areas which equal 3 and 5 parts

whole

6 Illusion and perception

When you embark on any kind of creative art it will not be long before you begin to realize what a deceiver the eye can be. Two-dimensional art uses this fact to its advantage and relies heavily on the eye being duped. Even the most simple assessments have to be carefully made to allow for this factor.

Your eye can be cheated to a remarkable degree. Here are a few simple examples of optical illusion.

Most people have difficulty in estimating the centre of a sheet of paper. If we measure it accurately it seems to be too low. The *visual* centre will be slightly higher than the *actual*, measured, centre. (Page 43)

Diagram A shows a piece of work mounted with equal measured margins, i.e. the work is exactly in the centre. You will see that it looks too low. A slightly wider margin at the bottom will rectify this effect, as shown in B.

Perhaps the most interesting use of illusion occurs in the application of *perspective*, that is the representation of objects *as we see them* in terms of size and position in space. (For example, an object viewed from a distance *appears* to be smaller than when it is viewed from close quarters.)

Each of the illustrations on page 45 shows the same figure. It is so far away in the first that it appears only as a speck in the distance. Gradually as it comes closer, it appears as a larger and larger image, with more recognizable details.

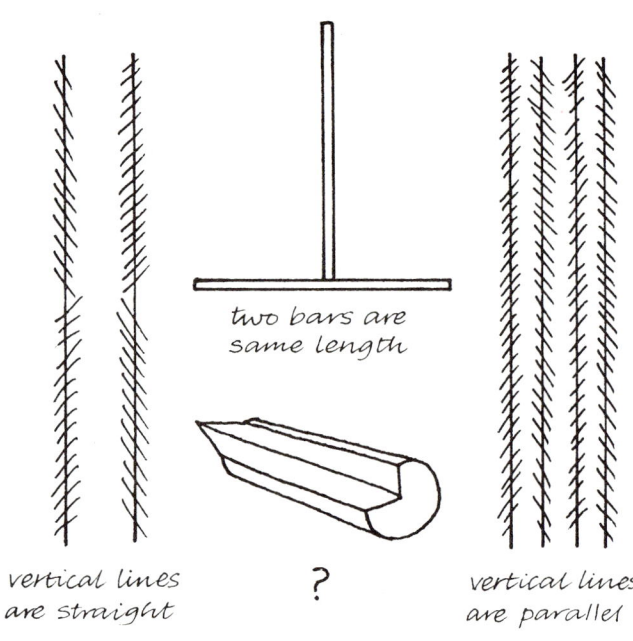

two bars are same length

vertical lines are straight

?

vertical lines are parallel

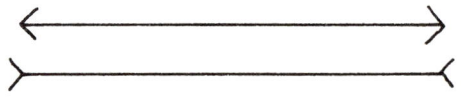

two lines are same length

Centres

Real centre line - looks too low

Visual centre line - looks correct -
(is slightly above real centre)

Margins

A

B

Work mounted with equal margins looks too low; bottom margin appears to be narrower than the other three.

Same work mounted with slightly wider margin at the bottom. Work appears to be in the centre of the mount.

Perspective

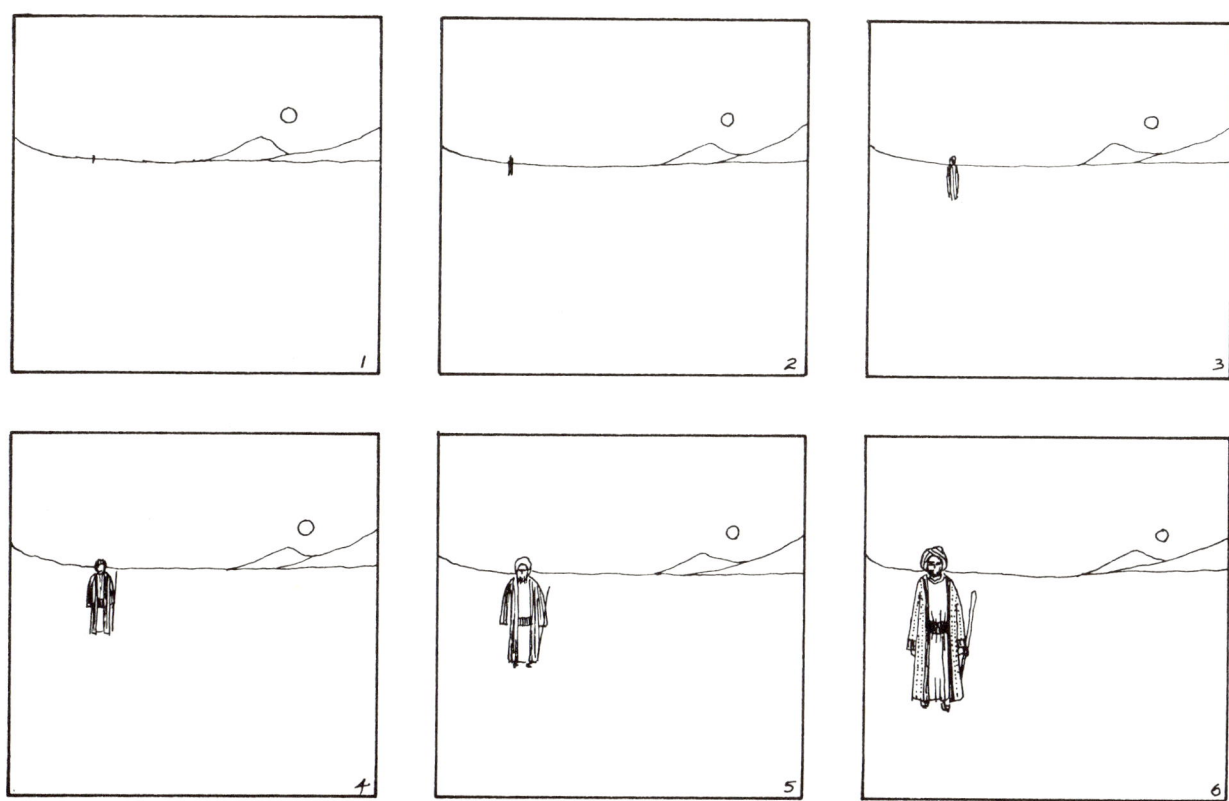

The same object viewed from different levels also presents differing images. The illustrations show the same figure viewed from three different levels. (The symbol of the eye represents the level of the viewer's eyes.)

<u>Line drawings</u>

Same thickness of line overall gives a flat appearance

Varied widths of line give emphasis and an illusion of depth

Perspective and its rules are a wide and complex subject and one on which many practical books are available. In its most complicated form it is used by technical illustrators and draughtsmen; in a simpler form by architects, interior designers and artists generally.

In real life no form has an outline around it. However, by using the device of *line* for drawing, we can indicate where one thing ends visually and another begins. If you look carefully at the drawings on page 47 you will see that the first has the same quality and thickness of line overall. The second illustrates how much more successful the drawing can be if the width and emphasis of line is varied, the parts nearest the viewer being in the heaviest line. This variation in emphasis creates an illusion of perspective.

The same applies to the use of tone. The farther away objects are, the lighter their tone can be to give the impression of perspective. The first sketch shows a scene with very little variation in tone. The second emphasizes the foreground with a heavy tone, and immediately an illusion of distance is established.

Use of tone to create illusion of depth

Colour can be used to create an illusion of distance in a similar way, using high-chroma colours in the foreground, gradually fading away into the distance to neutrals.

Errors in perspective can produce distortion of *scale*. Primitive art and the art of young children generally pays little attention to this factor (which often gives it its visual appeal). The illustration shows a child's portrayal of a scene with a house, woman and dog, out of scale. The second indicates the correct scale using the same units. However, the meaning of the images in the child's drawing is clear as they have become almost *symbols* of the real things.

Scale
Child's drawing using wrong scale.
In relation to house figure is too large,
dog is too large for figure. Relative heights:
house 25ft., figure 25ft., dog 20ft.

Same elements used
with correct scale.
Relative heights:
house 25ft., figure 5ft.,
dog 2ft.

49

Symbolism allows us to represent things by suggestion. It is especially useful in expressing ideas and emotions rather than actual objects. The examples show several of the more obvious traditional symbols.

Lines, or implied lines, which indicate directions for our eyes to follow, can supply a visual rhythm. The drawing of the ducks is made up of soft curves. These similar line shapes are in *harmony*. Even the implied lines echo the basic curves. Differing types of line, or implied line, provide a contrast in terms of rhythm (e.g. the soft round parts of a cactus plant as opposed to its spikes).

There are certain visual equivalents that we accept when we are translating the real, three-dimensional, world into two dimensions.

Overlapping objects can be suggested by showing only the visible portions of those objects and emphasizing where one passes in front of another.

We are able to see *through* certain materials, for instance glass, Perspex, water. If only the visible edge of an object is represented we can accept that it is transparent, providing the objects behind it are shown. For an *opaque* object (something we cannot see through), an impression of something solid is required. *Translucent* (semi-transparent) objects need a different approach; they are represented here by using a lighter emphasis of line and by altering the tone and, or, colour of the object seen behind the translucent material. Objects seen through a translucent material usually have an indistinct quality rather like an out-of-focus image.

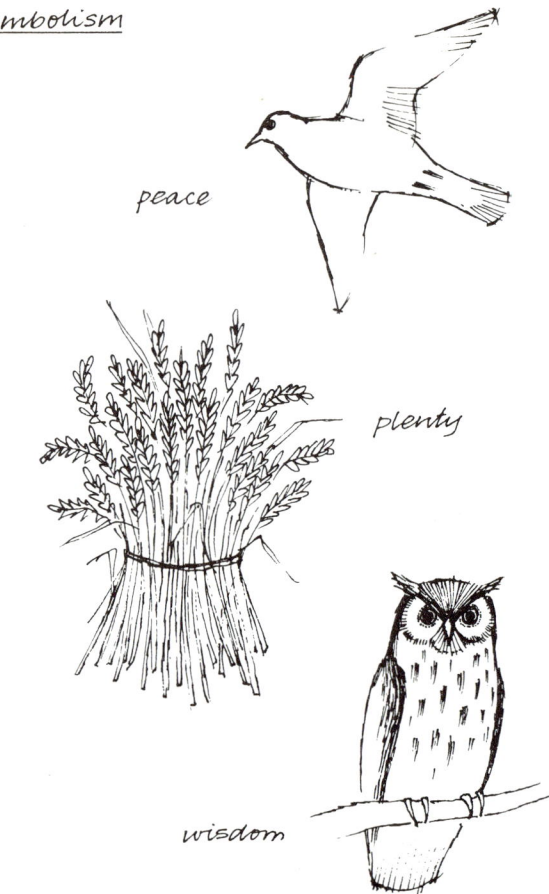

Symbolism

peace

plenty

wisdom

Line harmony

implied line

line

Line contrast

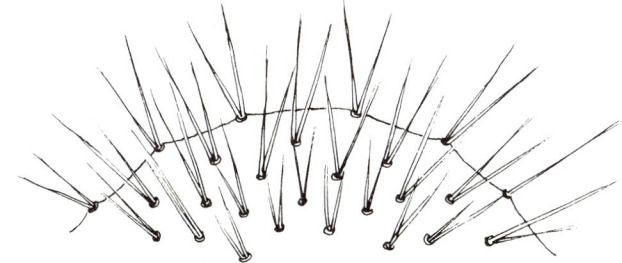

Overlapping

Transparency

Opacity

Translucency

Similarity

shape

form
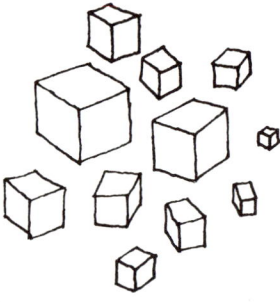

line
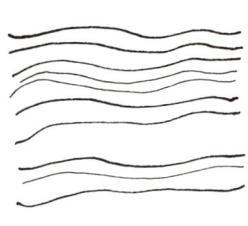

size

style

function

texture

rhythm

tone
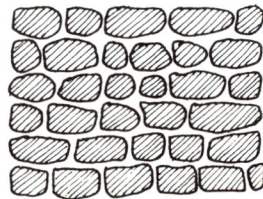

Contrast

shape

form

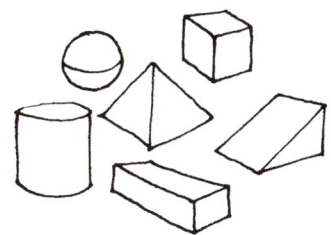

line

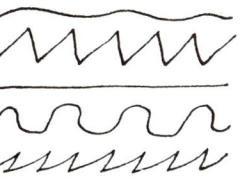

size

style

function

texture

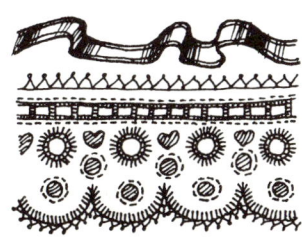

rhythm

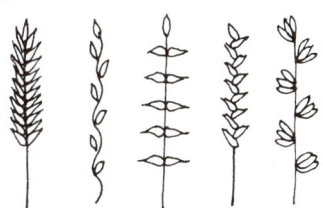

tone

53

The majority of visual art expressions are static, fixed for as long as they last in one position. However, *kinetic* art makes use of *motion* and can concern not only moving images, as in films, but moving forms. These may involve the use of such forces as electricity, magnetism, gravity and human energy.

There are many other phenomena and aspects of what we perceive (or understand through our senses) which can be translated into art. Examples are concavity (hollowness) and its opposite, convexity, and the qualities of similarity and contrast. Other aspects such as colour, tone, texture, shape and form, style and function, size and proportion have already been discussed in more depth in their respective chapters.

7 Drawing and sketching

No matter what kind of art or craft you are concerned with you will probably need the ability to draw and sketch.

Sketching is the shorthand used to record ideas; drawing is the equivalent of the typed manuscript.

Sketching is usually done very quickly with mere suggestions of line, shape, tone and possibly colour. Making a drawing is a more laborious procedure involving accurate measurements.

Pencil sketch

Compare the two illustrations, both made with a pencil and of the same subject. The sketch took only a few seconds, the drawing several hours.

Notice the serious, static quality of the drawing in relation to the light-hearted, free, quality of the sketch.

The sketch has one very important feature: it reduces shapes to a basic minimum. In this sense it is uncomplicated, while still expressing the artist's feelings about the subject. Sketching allows for mistakes: they are unimportant.

Pencil drawing

56

It does not detract from the value of the sketch that the cat has four tails. The artist has merely tried out the tail in three different positions. Several vague lines form the shapes but the inaccuracy does not matter.

There are many types of sketching and drawing. The illustrations show several of the more usual.

Graphic sketch

Confident, crisp style – strong basic shapes, no fussy details – glamourized and exaggerated – used for illustration and advertising

Sketching – mistakes do not matter

57

Cartoon – two meanings

a) Working sketch or tracing with information for finished work, either to a scale or actual size.

b) Humorous sketch – usually in a simple, personal style. Distortions of scale, proportion, mood and attitude are typical. There are standard ways of representing speech, thought, movement etc.

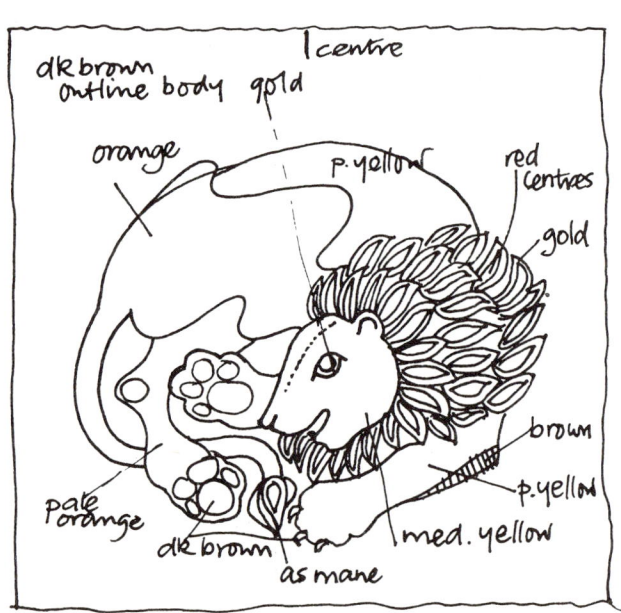

centre
dk brown outline body gold
orange
p. yellow
red centres
gold
pale orange
dk brown as mane
med. yellow
brown
p. yellow

help

Fashion sketch

Figure is suggested to show off main shape and details of style of clothes. Pose reflects mood of fashion. Note extra long neck, exaggerated height and slimness.

Working drawing

Drawn to a scale, it shows all the information needed to produce the finished article:

- design
- construction
- measurements
- materials
- instructions

The drawing, which is made with instruments, has a number, date and signature

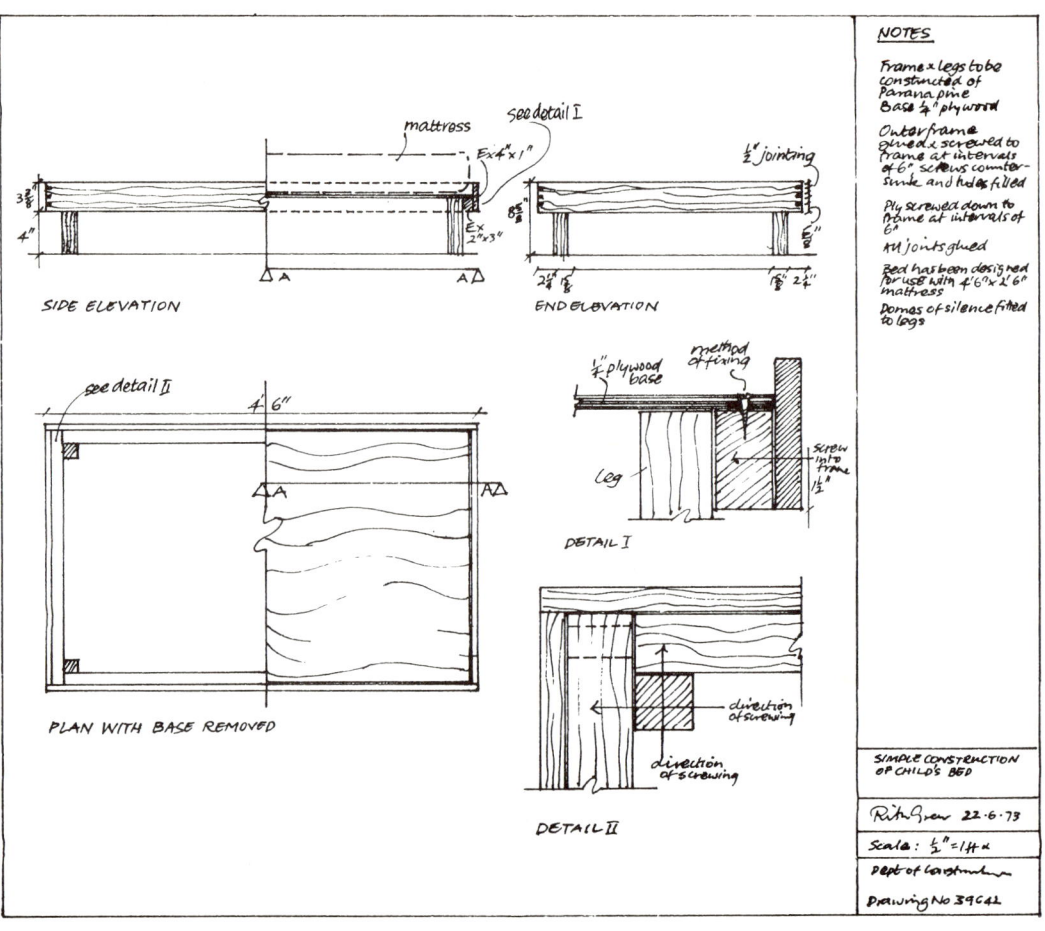

SIDE ELEVATION

mattress

see detail I

Ex 4"x1"

Ex 2"x3"

END ELEVATION

½" jointing

PLAN WITH BASE REMOVED

see detail II

4' 6"

DETAIL I

½" plywood base

method of fixing

Leg

screw into frame

DETAIL II

direction of screwing

direction of screwing

NOTES

Frame & legs to be constructed of Parana pine. Base ¼" plywood

Outer frame glued & screwed to frame at intervals of 6" screws countersunk and holes filled

Ply screwed down to frame at intervals of 6"

All joints glued

Bed has been designed for use with 4'6"x 2'6" mattress

Domes of silence fitted to legs

SIMPLE CONSTRUCTION OF CHILD'S BED

Rita Grew 22·6·73

Scale: ½"=1ft

Dept of Construction

Drawing No 39C42

Keeping a sketch book is rather like keeping a visual diary. It does not have to be a beautiful spiral-bound book with best quality cartridge paper. A collection of old envelopes and assorted paper fastened into a file serve just as well. Often the variation in the texture and colour of different papers make a useful contribution to effect.

Colour can be indicated either by brushed-on or crayoned-in areas or actual written notes. The illustration shows a sketch in which both colour and tone are denoted.

The basic advantage of sketching is that the result is not precious. Sketching is a quick, throw-away process for use in making other forms of art and recording information.

Sketch with tone and colour notes

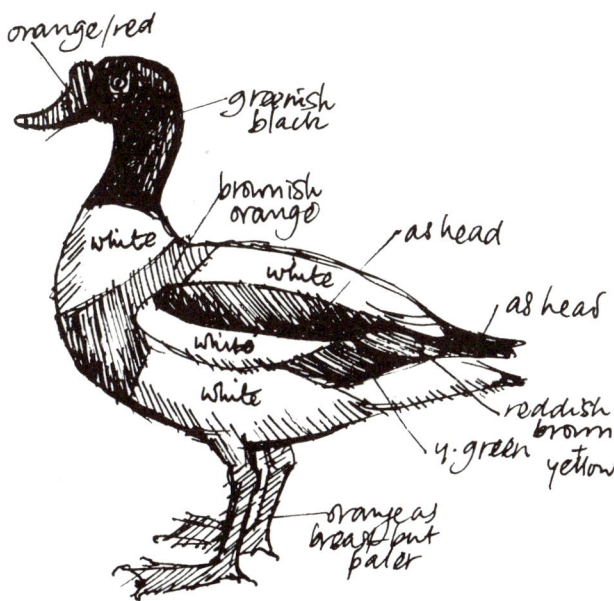

orange/red

greenish black

brownish orange

as head

white

white

as head

white

white

white

reddish brown

y.green

yellow

orange as breast but paler

A drawing is a series of measurements which make a kind of mathematical map. It is a record of assessments and decisions made by the artist, plus what he feels about the subject.

The drawing shown involves many measurements. Sometimes it is necessary to make several checking measurements to make sure the position of a particular point is correct.

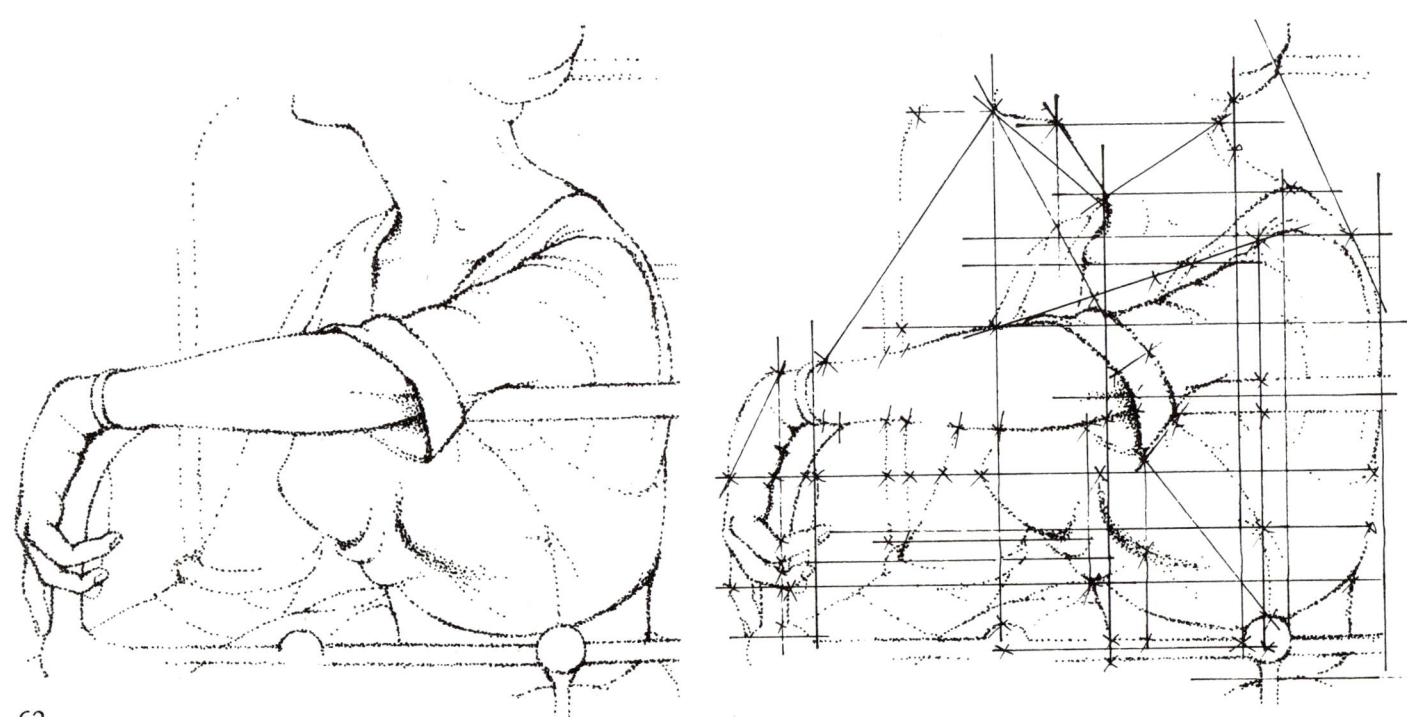

Fortunately most people have a reasonable idea of the horizontal and the vertical, and can make comparisons with a pencil to establish various angles.

The pencil should be held seven to ten inches away from the viewer's eye, as shown.

Assessing angles in this way is rather like making a scaffolding for the structure of the drawing. Equally important is the question of establishing relative size. Again a pencil is used, but this time held at arms length. The pencil is then used as a measure.

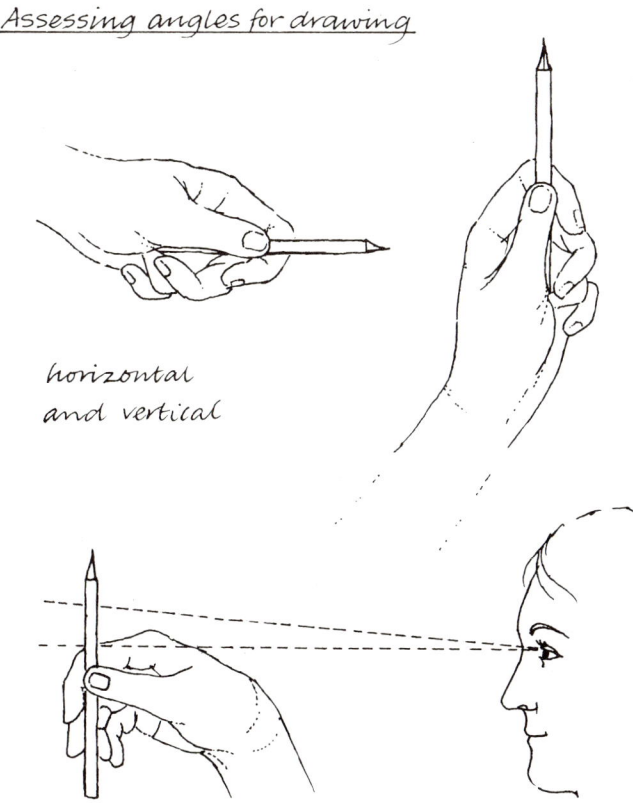

Assessing angles for drawing

horizontal and vertical

pencil held a few inches away from eye

Drawing 'sight size'

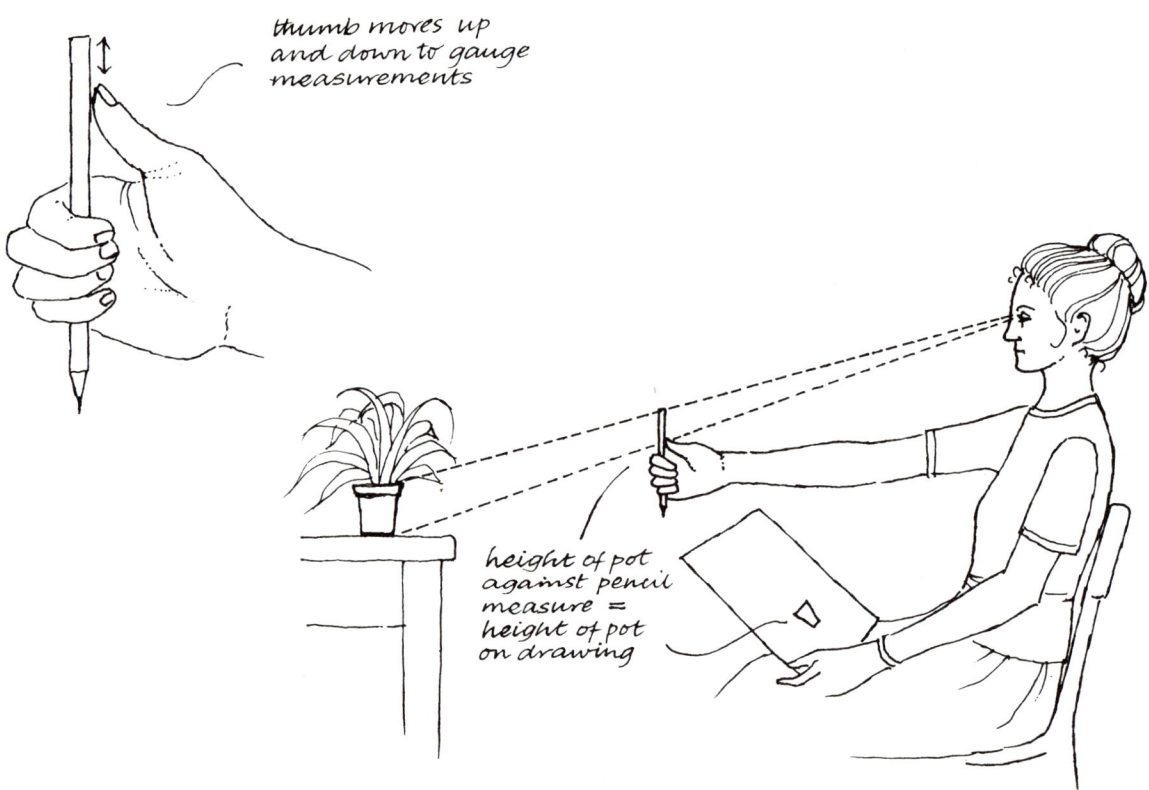

thumb moves up
and down to gauge
measurements

height of pot
against pencil
measure =
height of pot
on drawing

By holding the pencil with the fingers only the thumb can be moved up and down or along to gauge height or length.

NB   The hand holding the measuring pencil — don't use the same one for drawing — must always be held at the same distance from the body when a measurement is taken. If there is any variation, inaccuracy will undoubtedly result.

The objects drawn in this way will be what is called 'sight size', that is the size actually seen by the artist.

Many beginners find this method helps them to be accurate but it can become a lazy way of drawing and will halt improvement if leaned on too heavily. It is wiser to try to establish size by comparison: start with one measurement and try to find another one, equal in length, somewhere else.

As a person's drawing ability improves fewer measurements will need to be taken. The eye begins to take its responsibility more seriously and learns to make accurate judgements. This is what is meant by having 'a good eye'.

It is often difficult to make a distinction between what is a sketch and what is a drawing. Sometimes work can be both, when one part is worked in detail and the remainder merely sketched in.

The more accurate your eye becomes the more quickly you will be able to draw and the drawing itself is likely to be more spontaneous and lively, rather like a sketch.

When colour is used the need to indicate where one area ends and another begins by means of a drawn line does not arise: this is evident from the boundaries of the coloured areas. Nor is there when working in three dimensions: every part of a form has its own limits and where these occur either another form or a volume of space begins.

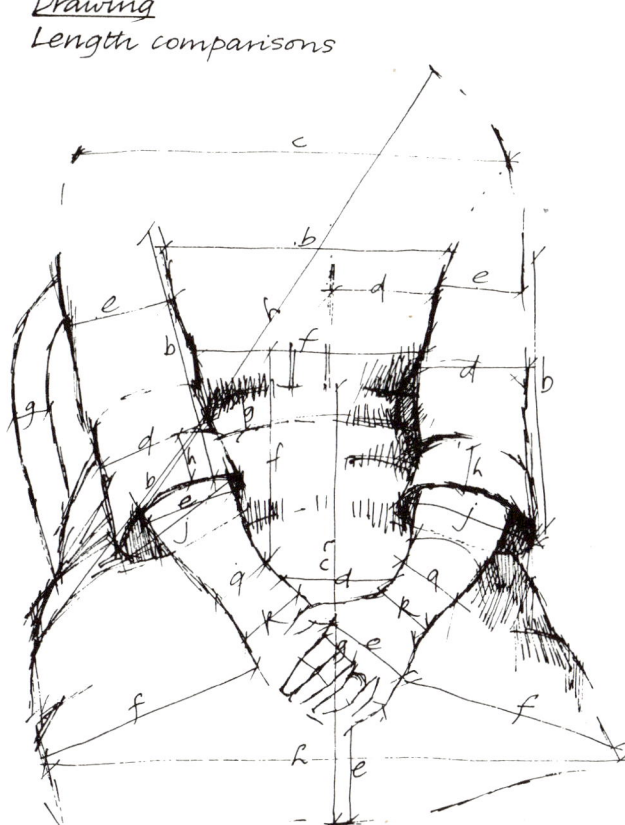

Drawing
Length comparisons

To sum up: drawing is not an easy process for most of us. Everyone will have some degree of talent or aptitude to call upon but even so drawing requires great concentration, effort and imagination. Difficulties which take a long time to overcome, lack of aim and the wrong attitude can lead to feelings of frustration and despair. Effort, though, is enormously rewarding in terms of visible progress and can lead to intense feelings of achievement and satisfaction — better described as exhilaration than mere pleasure.

The importance of a good teacher who knows when to advise and encourage is invaluable, but in the long run learning to draw is a meaningful personal struggle which may take a lifetime and still not be won.

8 Composition

Most forms of art and craft are composed of units arranged to make a whole (just as individual notes and chords are put together to make a piece of music). These arrangements, or compositions, can be made consciously, following a plan or design, or unconsciously as an instinctive process. Many factors need consideration when making a composition, the main ones being the behaviour of the eye and an understanding of visual balance.

To discuss composition we need to be aware of many facets of our general understanding and experience. The illustrations show various items of information we take for granted as being general knowledge. They form part of the basic vocabulary for understanding composition.

Basic concepts/ideas

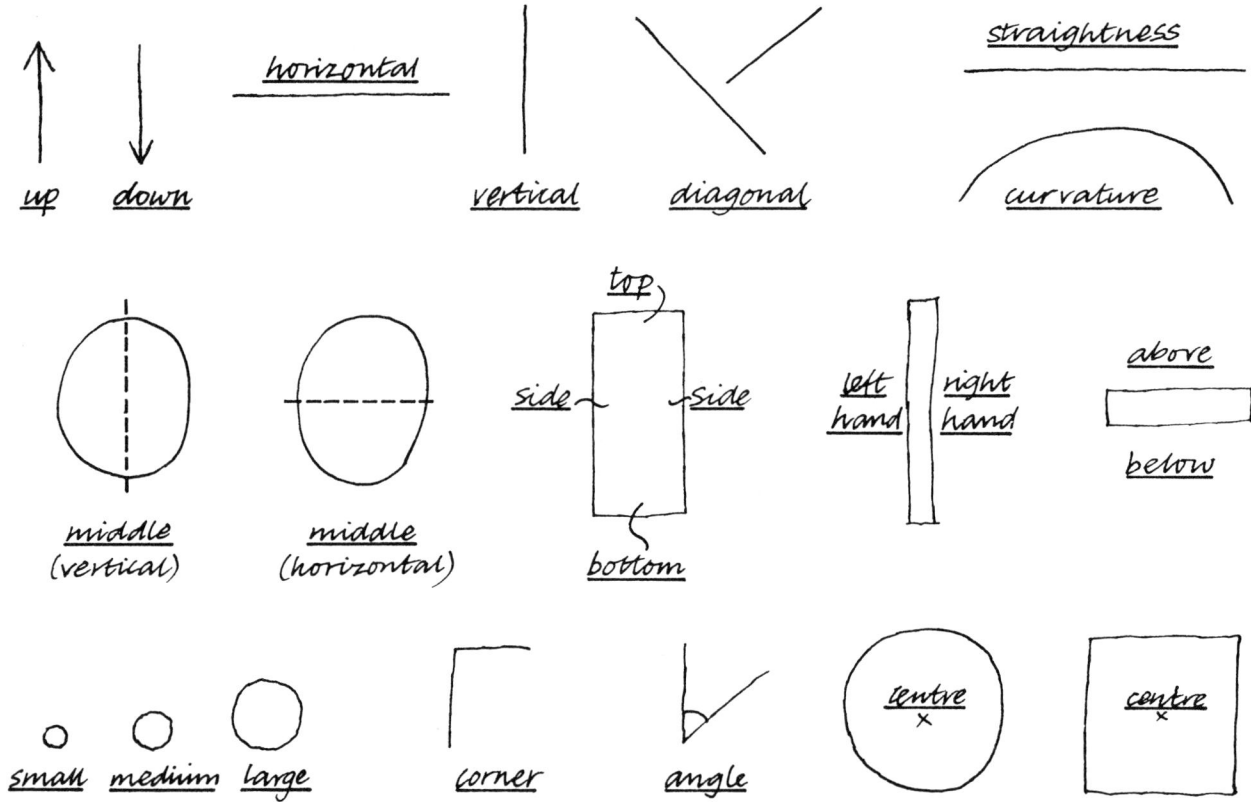

up   down

horizontal

vertical   _diagonal_

straightness

curvature

middle (vertical)   _middle_ (horizontal)

top

side   _side_

bottom

left hand   _right hand_

above

below

small   _medium_   _large_

corner

angle

centre ×

centre ×

Basic concepts/ideas

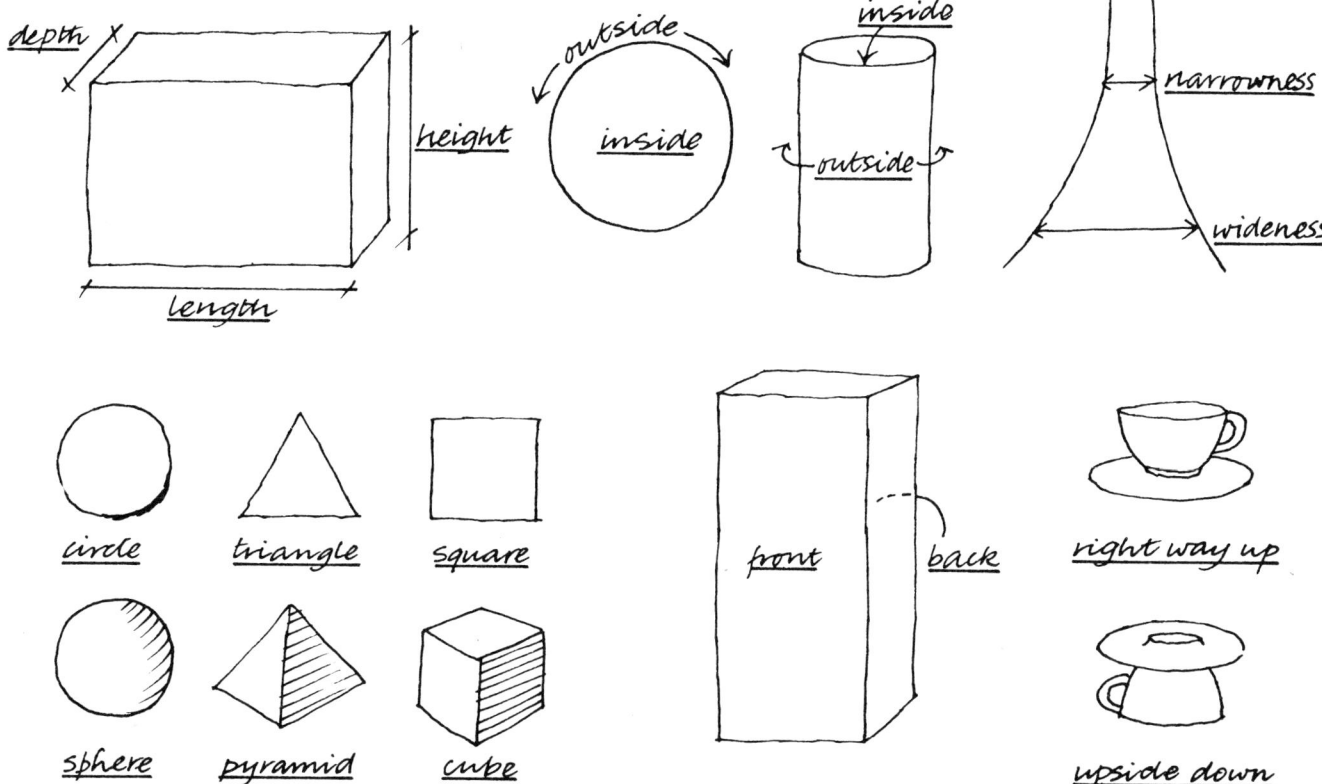

depth

height

length

outside

inside

inside

outside

narrowness

wideness

circle

triangle

square

sphere

pyramid

cube

front

back

right way up

upside down

When you look at an object your eyes wander about, taking in various details to build up an understanding of its form.

When your eye is confronted with several units, as in a painting, it does the same thing; it roves about, pausing on details, returning time and time again to one part. This is called the *focal point*, i.e. a part of the work which especially interests the eye.

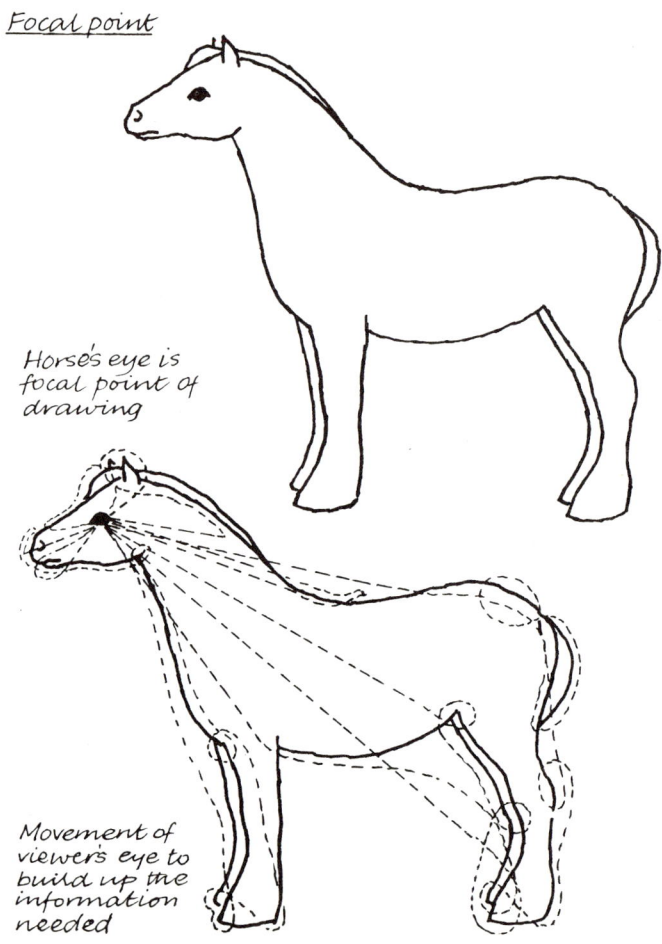

Focal point

Horse's eye is focal point of drawing

Movement of viewer's eye to build up the information needed

The artist usually knows from the outset what the focal point will be and constructs the whole work so that the other parts can be used to draw the eye to that point.

In most arrangements you will find that your eye will want to keep returning to one point, even if you try to avoid letting it do so. When you speak face to face with another person you generally look into one of his eyes and then the other, glancing from side to side. This is because the eye is the focal point of the face and there are two competing for your attention.

When looking at a three-dimensional form, such as a piece of sculpture, the focal point will probably be a three-dimensional unit although the precise point on which your eye wants to rest changes as your view of the object changes.

The focal point does not have to be an actual point; it can be quite a large area or form, or even, in some cases, a space. *Centre of interest* would really be a more suitable term.

By stimulating the movement of the eye, lines can be used to convey a feeling of movement in a particular direction. In this composition the centre of interest is the group of horsemen. Notice how several lines lead your eye to the figures.

Contrast in tone can also be used in the same way. The 'old master' portraits draw attention to the face by using an area of pale tone surrounded by dark tones. The use of an accent in a colour scheme will immediately attract the eye (e.g. a bright orange cushion on a black sofa). In a composition of large shapes a small shape can be used to attract the eye's attention by its contrast, and vice versa.

Composition – direction of line

Many lines lead the eye to the group of figures under the tree — the centre of interest

Focal points

Eyes present two focal points – viewer looks from one to the other.

Tone contrast

In contrast to area of dark tones, pale tone of face becomes centre of interest.

Centre of interest - contrasts

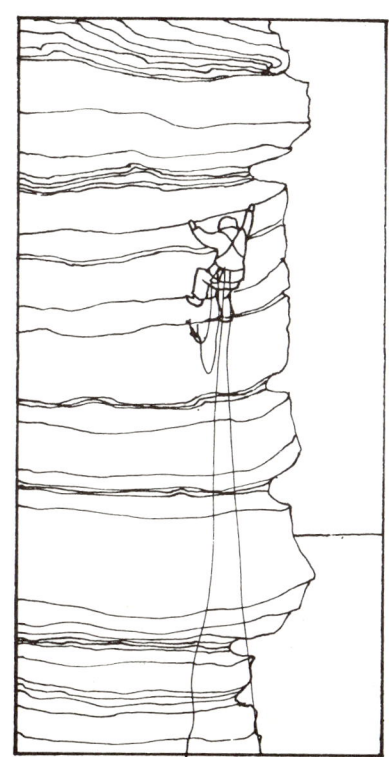

small shape/large shapes

large shape/small shapes

dark tone/light tones

curves/straight lines

straight lines/curves

73

Similarly, contrasts in shape may be used to good effect (e.g. straight lines opposed to curves).

The eye tends to divide complicated arrangements into units. The sketches show examples of this, and the illustrations which follow give several examples of *groups* of small units organized to form larger ones. The most effective way of grouping is probably by using colour, but it can also be achieved by 'proximity' or the nearness of areas and objects of the same size, colour shape and tone.

Small units form complicated arrangement

Eye breaks up arrangement into larger simplified units.

Grouping by colour

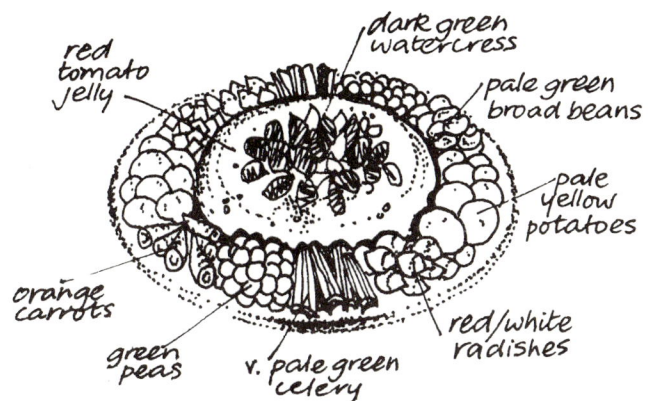

red tomato jelly

dark green watercress

pale green broad beans

pale yellow potatoes

red/white radishes

v. pale green celery

green peas

orange carrots

Grouping by proximity (nearness)

Grouping by similar size

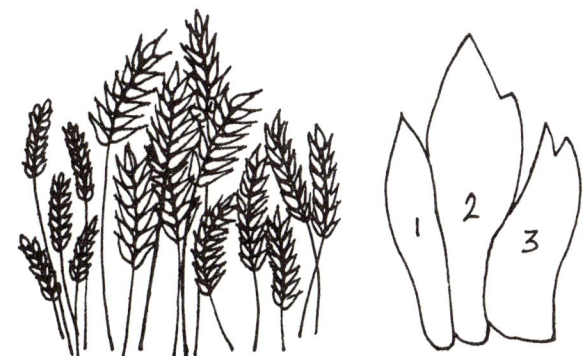

Grouping by similar shapes

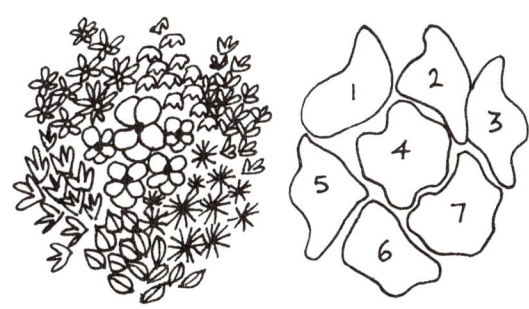

75

We do not usually see one unit in isolation if it is part of a whole arrangement. This means that the value of a unit tends to depend on the value of the remaining units in a composition (i.e. the value of a unit in a composition changes with the addition or subtraction of another unit). In the diagram on the opposite page the bird is exactly the same size in each composition. In the first it appears to be a large unit, in the second a small one. The tree appears as a light tone in the top diagram while in the bottom one it appears to be darker. In reality they are the same tone.

Grouping – by similar tone

Relative size

Relative tone

The birds are exactly the same size in each diagram

The trees are really the same tone in both diagrams

Very few people are without some sense of composition. The main difficulty beginners encounter is perhaps that of *balancing* units in an arrangement. As we tend to apply the natural laws of gravity to visual situations our understanding of gravity is often the measure for how successfully we do this.

If you could shake a sack of various sized flint pebbles, the heaviest and largest pebbles would fall to the bottom allowing the smaller ones to come to the top. A composition arranged on the same principle is usually more satisfactory than vice versa.

This variety of impossible balancing situations will probably make you feel uneasy. The illustration shows arrangements of identical units which are physically possible.

Gravity/experience

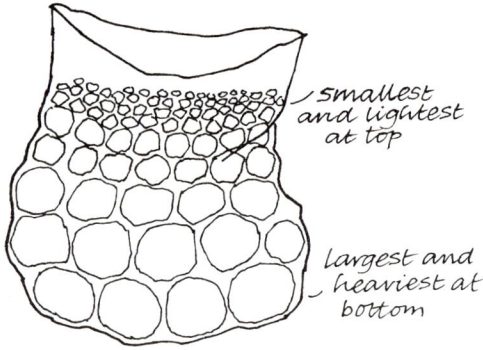

smallest and lightest at top

largest and heaviest at bottom

Natural situation

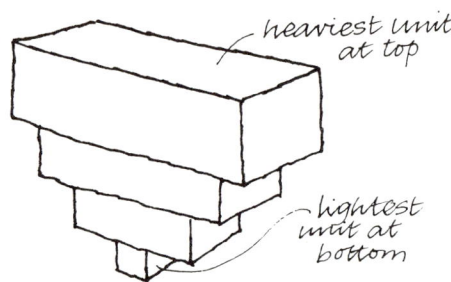

heaviest unit at top

lightest unit at bottom

Unnatural situation – units are well-balanced but viewer feels uneasy

Imbalance

Balance

Imbalance can give a feeling of falling which is why the dancer in the sketch appears to be keeling over. Similarly, heavy units arranged high in a composition will often give a pressing-down feeling. Strong lines may give a sense of direction which can encourage the eye to move right off the arrangement, and this too is an unsettling kind of imbalance.

Visual weight

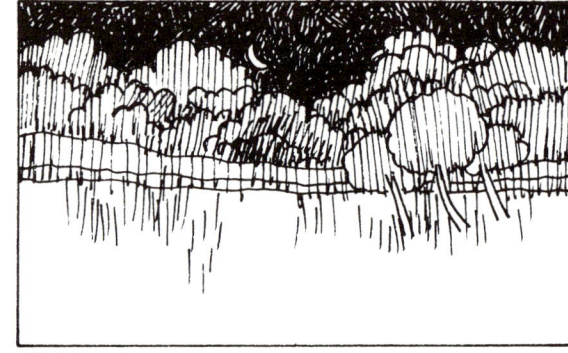

Heavy tone at top gives pressing down feeling

Direction

Lines lead the eye right out of composition

80

In spite of all these points there are, surprisingly, only two basic types of unit arrangement. These involve the use of *symmetry* and *asymmetry*. The test for these two types of arrangement is to divide an object down the middle with an imaginary line. Symmetrical objects will then present two matching, or almost matching halves, and asymmetrical ones will have totally different halves.

<u>Symmetry</u>
One half mirrors the other

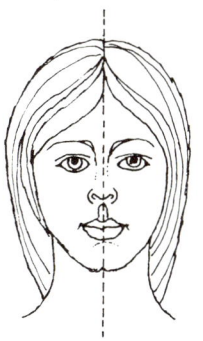 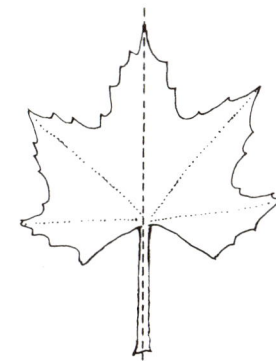

<u>Asymmetry</u>
Halves are different

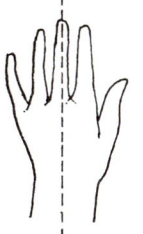 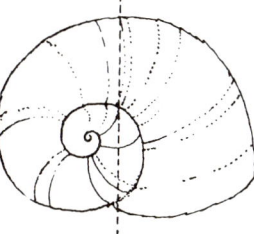

Although asymmetry is more difficult to manage, most people find this type of composition more satisfying. The illustrations show two compositions made up of similar units. There is something rather dull about the symmetrical arrangement of the top one, the bottom one being far more interesting and visually acceptable.

The following illustrations give an indication of the more usual errors beginners make in composition, with corrections.

These errors would not have occurred had the person making the drawing used a sketch plan. This method is especially useful for beginners because it gives a definite shape for the final work and indicates at the outset the size and shape of the paper that will be needed.

Symmetrical composition

Asymmetrical composition — same units

<u>Composition</u> – common errors (top line) and corrections (bottom line)

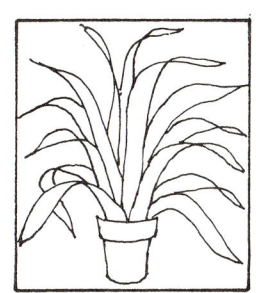

drawing is too
large for paper

figure dropping out
of picture

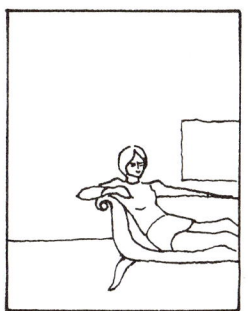

no room for legs
and feet

no room for feet

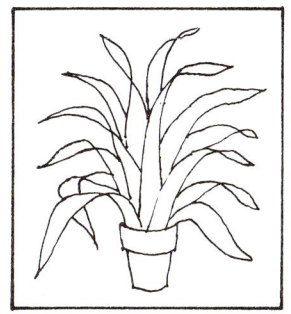

larger size of paper
used

figure raised

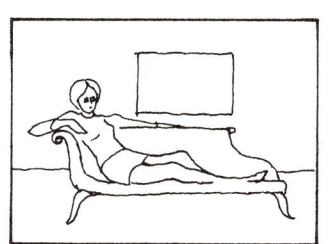

turn paper round

figure raised

If a quick sketch is made of the subject matter and a frame drawn round it, this will indicate the *shape* of the paper needed.

To transfer the sketch to the full-size paper divide both the sketch and the paper into four to find the centre of each. This will give you a good guide for positioning the finished drawing. (See page 102 for a more detailed description of how to transfer and enlarge preliminary sketches.)

Experienced artists are able to arrange compositions instinctively, but when instincts let the artist down, as they sometimes do, he must consciously make judgements about the value of the units involved, to see where he has made a mistake. He will say 'It doesn't work', or 'There is something wrong', because he feels uneasy about the arrangement.

The sketches on pages 85 and 86 show how a composition can be built unit by unit, and how the eye's behaviour must be considered.

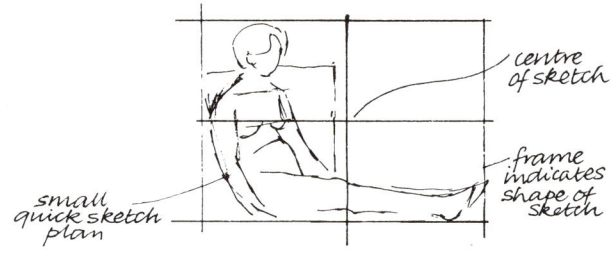

centre of sketch

frame indicates shape of sketch

small quick sketch plan

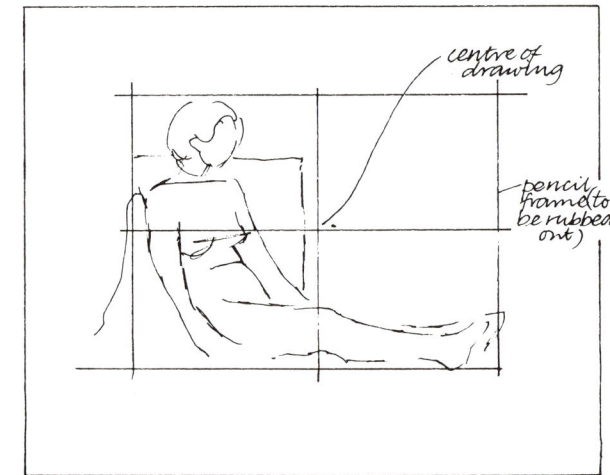

centre of drawing

pencil frame (to be rubbed out)

Basis of final drawing correctly positioned

Making a balanced composition, unit by unit

(arrows and dotted lines indicate direction of eye)

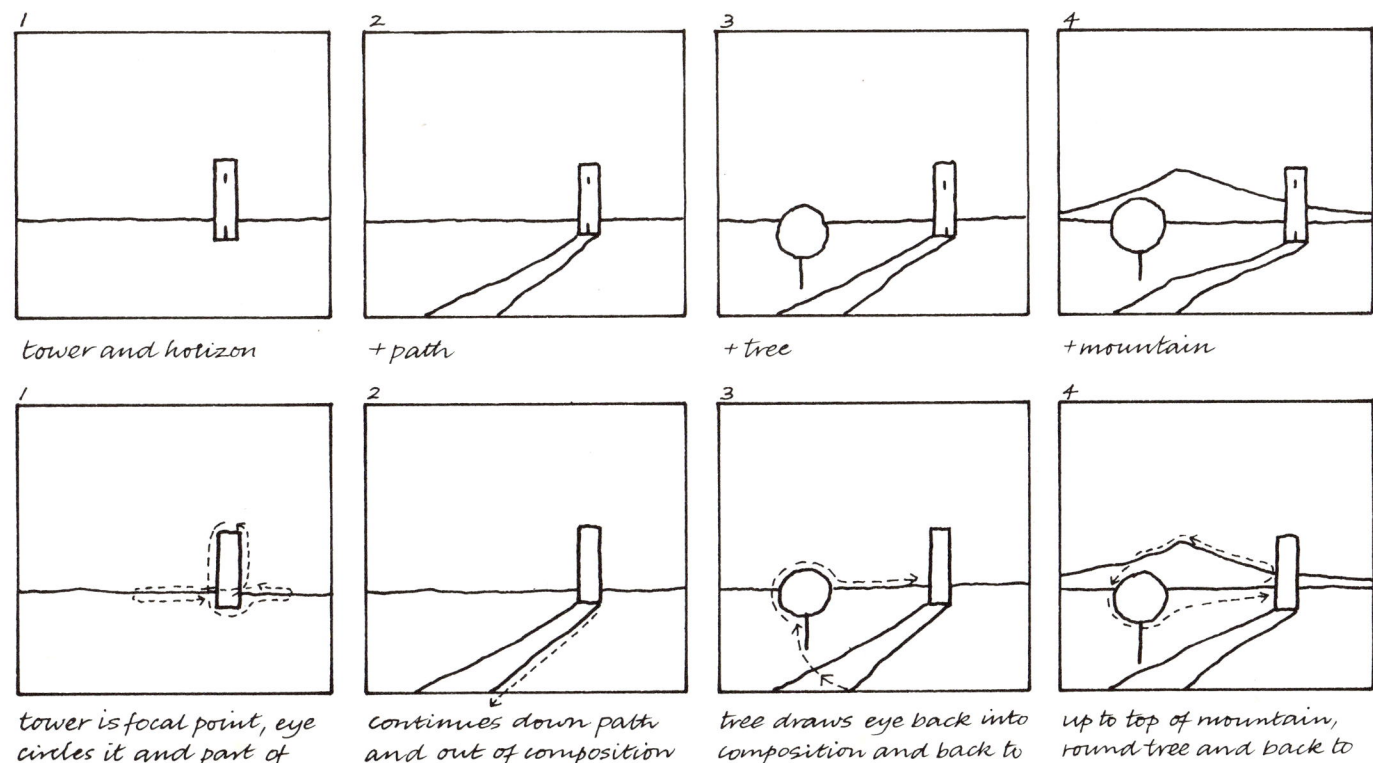

1 tower and horizon

2 + path

3 + tree

4 + mountain

1 tower is focal point, eye circles it and part of horizon

2 continues down path and out of composition

3 tree draws eye back into composition and back to focal point again

4 up to top of mountain, round tree and back to focal point

Making a balanced composition, continued

(Number 8 is completed composition)

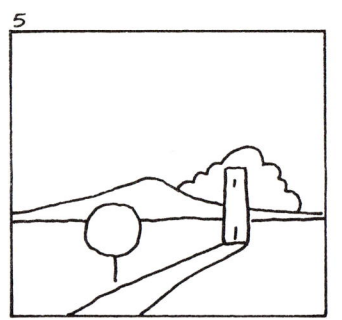

+ cloud behind tower

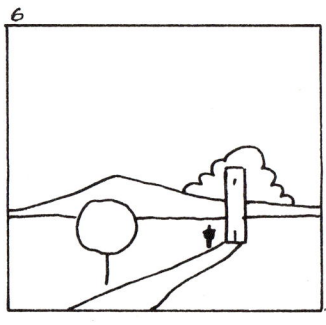

+ figure by tower

+ sun behind cloud

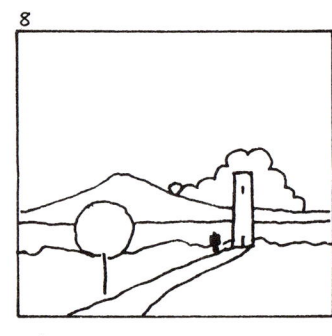

+ line at base of tower

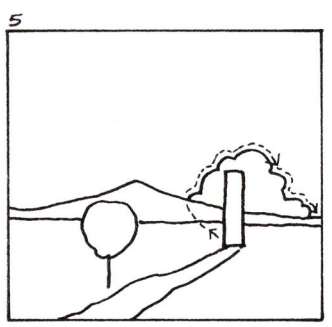

around cloud, down to
horizon and almost
out of composition

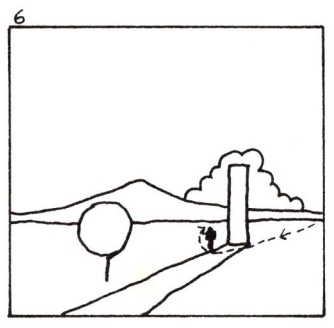

figure draws eye back

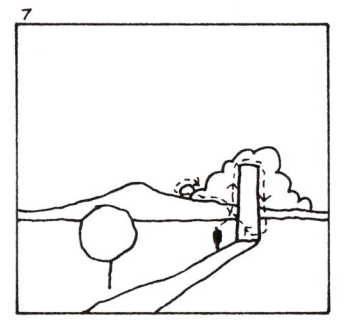

round focal point again
and up mountain to
sun

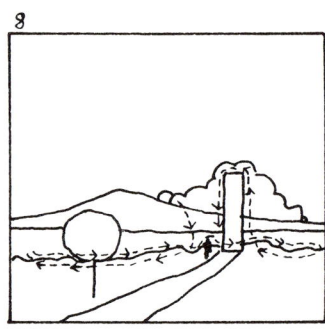

down to new line, along to
tree, across to edge and
back again to tower

The world would be very dull if all art were perfectly balanced and arranged. Sometimes imbalance is used to good effect. The next two sketches show different approaches to a similar landscape of trees. A is a well-balanced view of the subject with an almost comfortable arrangement of trees and sky. B has a large weight of trees at the top giving a strong feeling of menace and possibly danger.

There is no mysterious process involved in composition. It is merely the arranging of units to form a whole. However, the many factors that may be involved make it seem a complicated process, and one which the novice often finds difficult to understand. Those who do experience this difficulty can console themselves with the knowledge that serious study, practice and good guidance should answer the problem.

Composition and mood

Comfortable arrangement of trees, sky etc. indicate a summer day, peaceful & warm

Trees at top of composition give a feeling of menace, especially as heavy tones are used

9 The creative process

The creative process is very complex. It involves skill, experience, motivation, talent, imagination, the influences of personality and above all inspiration.

'What inspires you?' is a very familiar question to an artist. To outsiders, inspiration seems to be a magic formula for making art, but it is really the *influence* of someone or something on the artist. It is not always easy for us to say exactly what inspires us because we are not always aware of an influence in our lives, good or bad. Much depends on the culture in which we live, our geographical location and our own particular personality. For example, a tribesman living in the Sahara Desert will not produce the same kind of art as an Eskimo living in the Arctic wastes. They belong to entirely different cultures and are therefore influenced by entirely different phenomena.

The illustrations show the difference between two horses used as models. The first is from Mongolia and has a long body, short legs and small feet. The second is from Arabia and has long legs, powerful haunches and small head. The two artists who sculpted and painted the horses were influenced by what they understood a horse to be from their own experience of life.

<u>Influence/inspiration</u>

Horse from Arabian desert —
long legs, powerful haunches,
small head — used as model
for decorative painting

Horse from steppes of
Mongolia — long body,
short legs, small feet —
used as model for
sculpture

89

It is usually a stubborn person who finds it difficult to experience inspiration — someone whose mind is not open to new thinking and the idea of progress. To be influenced, the mind must be exposed and allowed to react accordingly. Depending on how strongly the influence is felt, *ideas* form in the mind.

To have an idea means to have a mental plan or pattern. 'I have no idea', or 'I don't know where to begin', really mean 'I have no plan to follow'.

Most of us are capable of employing ideas — whether our own or someone else's — by *translating* them into a particular art form. Even if an idea is not original, a person's interpretation of it may well be. However, if someone else's idea is to be used, it must be understood to be of any use. For example, a craftsman wishing to make a knife of any kind must understand the basic idea of a knife before he can attempt to design a new one. He knows immediately his task concerns a blade and handle, the established concept of a knife.

One example of the successful outcome of the translating process is the Bayeux Tapestry which succeeds in turning actual events (the Norman Conquest) into embroidery. The designers were influenced by what they saw and what they were told. This gave them a basic idea which could be interpreted for the tapestry. The shapes used are very simple and economic, perfectly suitable for needlework.

Some people have a natural aptitude for this translating process, and the ability to look at a complex object and see it immediately in terms of simple shapes. The same shapes, however, are there for all to see and for those without this gift it is a question of learning to see them.

When an artist signs his work he is indicating that it is primarily his *idea* rather than his technical organization of

90

Translation

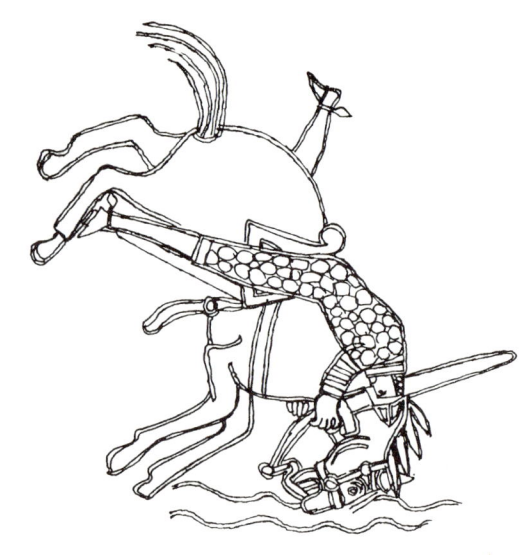

Actual event translated into simple shapes for needlework (Bayeux Tapestry)

material, which could have been done by anyone with parallel skill. (Many an 'old master' painting was in reality painted by apprentices, enabling the master painter to put forward a greater number of ideas.)

With the majority of crafts, the idea for work is probably a traditional one and the main feature is in the execution of the craft by an individual putting forward his own interpretation of the basic theme, or idea. This often occurs where the functional aspect of an object is of prime importance, as it is with a table or a spoon. Any new tables or spoons can only be a variation of the *original idea* of both.

As human beings we have many ways of expressing ourselves. Some are spontaneous, like smiling and crying. These expressive reactions occur and vanish, lasting only a few moments. More intelligible communication involves the use of spoken language. To preserve speech we can use mechanical ways of recording it in writing and sound. Feelings cannot be preserved in this way, but it is possible to make them recur by stimulating the senses.

Every work of art is an expression of feeling, for art is the language of emotion. When we look at something we find beautiful it gives us a feeling of pleasure. Some art we may find disturbing to the point of revulsion. (There is no law which says art has to be beautiful.) Each time we experience art it affects our emotions and we respond and react according to our instincts.

It is not only with our visual sense that we respond to art, our other senses can be employed too — taste, touch, hearing and smell. Art is not only painting, drawing and sculpture. These are probably the most lasting and important as records of expression, but art does not have to be lasting. Cooking, an arrangement of flowers, a laid table, can all be expressions of art.

In this age of automation many crafts have almost died, but others have become more important. Interest and emphasis change as art takes on new directions from the changes in society.

The following list gives some idea of the number of ways in which art is expressed today, through the fine arts, crafts and design for industry.

The Fine Arts Painting, drawing, sculpture.

Crafts Pottery and glassware, fabric printing and weaving, bookbinding, leatherwork, lettering and calligraphy, woodwork, silversmithing and jewellery.

Homecrafts Sewing and embroidery, toymaking, basketry, soft furnishing, flower arranging, cookery.

Design for industry Dress and fashion, woven and printed fabrics, pottery and glassware, interiors, furniture, graphics, advertising, television and films.

It is interesting to note the role of the amateur, or non-professional, in keeping alive crafts which otherwise might have died out due to lack of stimulus and interest.

To acquire and keep a skill needs hard work and application, but it is important to remember that too much emphasis on technique and materials can swamp the artist's originality of expression. Technique should be thought of merely as scaffolding.

Man is by nature a very restless and progressive animal, never satisfied for long. Fortunately he has the instinct to create things and so express himself, thus recording what he feels at a particular point in time. His art might be described as 'frozen feeling'; ideas transformed from thoughts into forms and images.

10 Materials and techniques

The process of producing any kind of work of art or craft is either 'additive' or 'subtractive'. We either add units or material to make a whole or we subtract them to leave the finished work. Some art activities employ both methods in turn.

The following tables relating to a selection of the more widely-practised arts and crafts give an indication of the tools and materials employed, the dimensions and processes involved, and some of the specialized aspects of those crafts.

Sometimes money is wasted on materials which are too good or not good enough, or buying expensive small quantities. Although materials and techniques are important, the end product must never be overshadowed by them; they are merely the scaffolding for the final work.

Examples of art and craft

Art or craft	dimensions	Tools/equipment for:	Materials	End product	Specialisation
Bookbinding	3	cutting, tooling stitching, punching	paper, card, vellum, leather, cloth, cord, adhesives, gold leaf	decoratively bound books	tooled leather work lettering, gilding
Canework	3	cutting, shaping bending	cane, wooden bases, handles, fastenings, frames	mats, trays, baskets, furniture	decorative weaving
Cookery	3	cutting, cleaning, mixing, blending, heating, baking, displaying	raw foodstuffs	edible food	diets and nutrition, cake icing, confectionery, preserves Cordon Bleu
Drawing/sketching	2	marking e.g. pencil, pen etc. drawing board	paper, card, media	drawings or sketches	portraits, landscapes figures, plants
Dressmaking (Needlework/sewing)	3	cutting, marking measuring, stitching, fitting	fabrics, leathers, trimmings, fastenings	garments for wear	fashion designing pattern cutting, decoration, tailoring
Embroidery	3 (low relief)	cutting, sewing measuring	fabrics, threads, beads, trimmings	decoration for garments, panels, pictures	Ecclesiastical work Gold work, collage, beadwork
Flower arranging	3	cutting, bending	containers, supports, drapes, plant materials	arrangements based on theme for setting	preservation, Ikebana, styles, collage
Glass	3	cutting, shaping moulding, blowing, grinding heating	sand + chemicals	glassware for use and decoration	cutting, engraving

Art or craft	dimen-sions	Tools/equipment for:	Materials	End product	Specialisation
Graphics	2	(drawing instruments and board) marking, measuring, painting photography	paper, card, media, photographic work	illustrations, advertising material	packaging design commercials (film) cartoons, photography advertising commercial art
Jewellery	3	cutting, shaping soldering, casting, polishing	silver, gold, copper precious and other stones, wood, plastics	jewellery for wear	enamelling fine jewellery (gems) costume jewellery
Lace	3 (low relief)	cutting, marking, winding, making (pillow) weaving	yarns, threads	lace motifs trimmings, inserts	tatting, crochet
Leatherwork	3	sewing, fixing, punching, tooling	leather skins, fastenings, thread, adhesives	leather goods for personal use.	luggage, gloves, gifts
Lettering and calligraphy	2	measuring, marking, brushing inking, painting	paper, card, vellum pigments, gesso, gold leaf	commercial lettering, signboards, scrolls, books, coats of arms	gilding, illuminating, ticket writing signwriting, heraldry
Lino cutting	2/3	cutters, gouges, pressing, rollers	lino, inks, paper card.	(printed) design capable of repetition.	book illustration
Painting	2	brushing, spreading	paper, canvas, paints	painting	water colours, oils, portraits, landscapes, still-life, abstracts,
Paper sculpture	3	marking, cutting shaping, fixing	paper, card, adhesives	sculpture (flimsy) for display, lampshades	exhibition work

Examples of art and craft continued

Art or craft	dimensions	Tools/equipment for:	Materials	End product	Specialisation
Pottery	3	shaping, moulding wheel, kiln	clay, glazes	pottery of all kinds for use and decoration	painted decoration
Photography	2	cameras, lights printing and processing, measuring, cutting, mounting	film, chemicals, water, printing paper	photographs, black & white and colour, transparencies	portraits, fashion, news, commercial, industrial
Screen printing	2	screen, squeegy	inks, dyes, paper, fabric	(printed) design for repetition, fabrics, wallpaper, fine art prints	posters, graphics,
Sculpture	3	cutting, shaping, carving, moulding	clay, stone, wood plaster, metals, plastics	fine art sculpture	bas or low relief portrait busts, statues architectural decoration
Soft toymaking	3	cutting, sewing bending, fixing	fabrics, leathers, stuffings, fittings, trimmings	soft toys	
Weaving	3	cutting, winding, knitting, looms	yarns, threads	woven or knitted cloth, garments, bedspreads	hand knitting hand weaving rugs, lace
Wood engraving	3/2	cutting, gouging, pressing	wood blocks, inks, paper	engravings, illustrations	book illustration
Woodwork and carpentry	3	marking, cutting, shaping, fixing, finishing, carving	woods, composition boards, fastenings, fittings	furniture, ornaments, fittings	carving, lettering, cabinet making, inlay

Paper

There are many different types of paper on sale for sketching and drawing which often leads to confusion.

The following are papers suitable for sketching:

1 *Bank paper* Very thin, slightly transparent, white, available in large pads or loose-leaf (typing paper), (A4), inexpensive
2 *Bond paper* Really meant for typing and writing, but excellent for drawing, small (A4 and under), used in a ring binder it makes a good cheap sketchbook; very white, smooth
3 *Cartridge* Good quality, heavy, cream or white, slightly textured, sold in expensive books or pads, or by the sheet, A1, A2, etc
4 *Brown paper* Wrapping paper, very strong and cheap, smooth one side, textured on the other.

The following are papers suitable for drawing:

1 *Bond paper*
2 *Cartridge paper*
3 *Sugar paper* Textured, apt to tear, available in dull colours, size A2 and down
4 *Brown puper*

For tracing the following papers are recommended:

1 *Toilet paper* Transparent tissue, very strong, cheap
2 *Greaseproof paper* Available in rolls or folded sheets, cheap
3 *Tracing paper* Expensive, good quality paper, strong, sold in large rolls

A good general-purpose paper is decorator's lining paper. This is incredibly cheap and, in the better qualities, is suitable for drawing. As it is sold in wide rolls it is ideal for large work.

Media for use with paper

1 *Pencil* Graded according to hardness of centre. B = black (soft), H = hard; gives a grey mark; can be erased; 6B for quick broad work which may need to be fixed with a spray to prevent smudging; 2B for broad sketching; HB for precise drawing; 2H for use on tracing paper.

2 *Charcoal* Very soft, smudgy and difficult to use; for large quick work; must be fixed (sprayed); available in pencil form; cannot be erased.

3 *Wax crayon* Basic range of colours; gives textured imprecise line; cannot be erased.

4 *Pen and ink* Mapping pens give a good variation of line, very precise and demanding, very good for drawing; indian ink looks rather dead; coloured inks available in a basic range, sepia or neutral tint good for drawing; areas of tone can be washed in with a brush; a strong medium which cannot be erased.

5 *Ink and watercolour* Use waterproof ink and lightly applied washes of watercolour; gives a softer more delicate effect than coloured ink.

6 *Paint and brush* There are many types of paint available but the most generally useful is opaque poster paint (gouache), sold in jars or tubes, mixed with water. Good ranges of colours in several makes and sizes. Watercolour — a transparent medium, gentle but difficult to use; mix generously with water. *Brushes* Sable are best but expensive; ox hair quite good; squirrel has no spring and is limp and lifeless.

7 *Felt-tip pens* contain coloured ink; very useful for quick sketching; give a loose woolly line; cannot be erased.

8 *Ballpoint pen* cannot be erased; available in a good black with a fine point; inexpensive, precise but inclined to smudge.

To stick paper and card

For sticking paper and card Cow Gum is excellent. It can be rubbed off with a 'rubber' made of used particles. Follow maker's instructions for use. Available in large tubes or economical tins; spread with a spatula or piece of card, never a brush.

Media

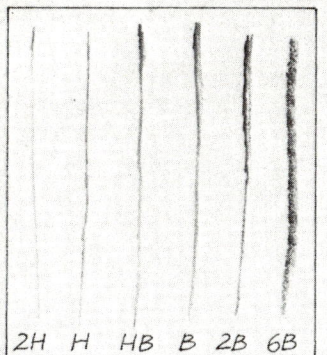

2H H HB B 2B 6B

Pencil

Charcoal

Wax crayon

Pen, ink and brush

Ink and watercolour

Paint and brush

Felt-tip pen

Fine ballpoint pen

Methods of reproducing two-dimensional units

Tracing direct

Use transparent paper and pencil. Place paper over design and trace. Remove paper and *turn over*. Scribble (as shown) over the traced design (preferable to drawing a thick line). Make sure all the necessary parts are covered. Turn over and place on clean paper. Draw over the design, using a fine point biro or hard pencil. A tracing may be used several times but after each time the back must be scribbled over again.

Making a template

Use only for very simple designs. Draw design on thin card and cut out with scissors or cutting knife. Position template on paper and draw round it holding pencil *vertically* as shown. A template can be used many times depending on how long the card lasts. Use a very sharp pencil for accuracy. N.B. A template drawing is always slightly *larger* than the template.

Making a stencil

Use for very simple designs. Draw shape on thin card and cut it out leaving a hole. Draw inside the shape holding the pencil vertically. A stencil can be used many times. A stencil drawing is always slightly *smaller* than the stencil.

Tracing

design to be reproduced

H pencil or fine ballpoint

tracing paper over design

clean paper

tracing turned over and scribbled on back

line carefully and firmly drawn over tracing

H pencil or fine ballpoint

100

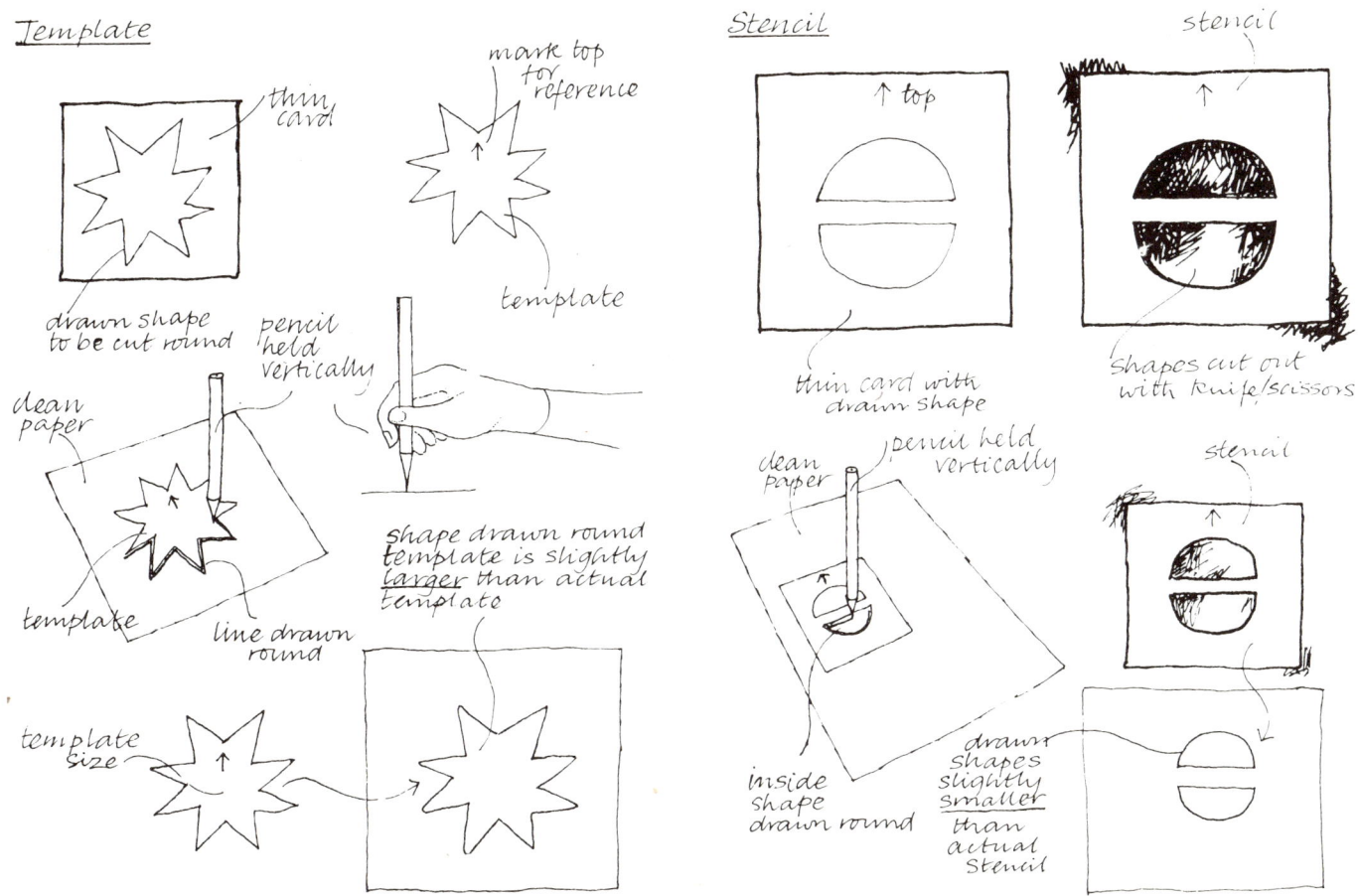

Template

thin card

drawn shape to be cut round

mark top for reference

template

clean paper

pencil held vertically

template

line drawn round

shape drawn round template is slightly larger than actual template

template size

Stencil

↑ top

stencil

thin card with drawn shape

shapes cut out with knife/scissors

clean paper

pencil held vertically

stencil

inside shape drawn round

drawn shapes slightly smaller than actual stencil

Enlarging - by reference grid

enlargement plotted, using grid for reference

drawing to be
enlarged

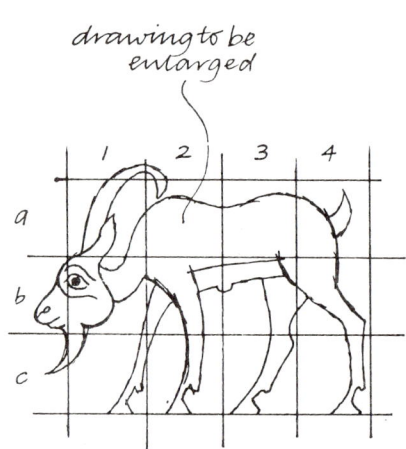

scaffold of squares over
drawing, marked for
reference

pencil grid to be rubbed out
after use

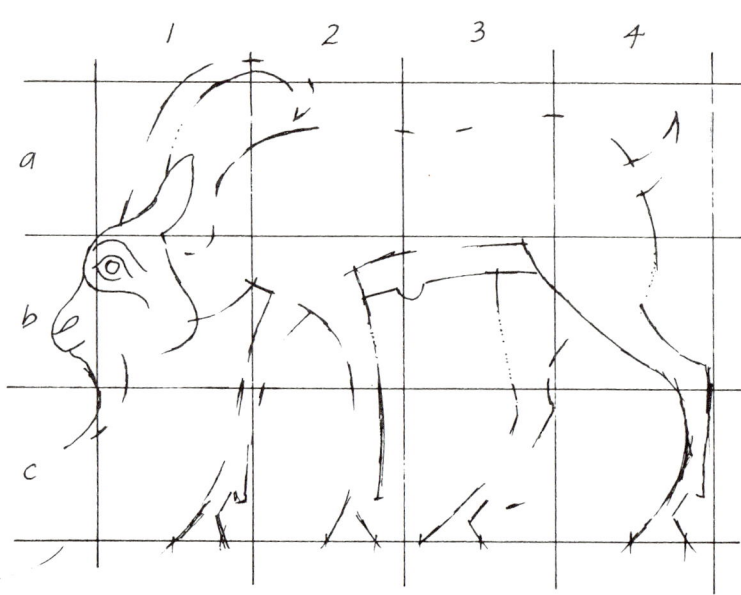

scaffold of larger squares, marked 1, 2, 3 & a, b, c etc
in the same way as smaller version

Enlarging

Enlarging a sketch accurately can be done quickly and simply by mechanical means.

Draw a scaffold over the sketch to give a frame of reference. Draw a larger frame in the same way. Plot in the motif on the larger scale as shown. Use square or circular frameworks as suitable.

The methods described provide quick and easy ways of repeating shapes, but if not used with great care they can be as inaccurate as free-hand sketching. It is attention to detail which is the test of the true craftsman. A superbly finished work of any kind must be composed of such details. A person who has the patience and the ability to do trivial things well will very likely arrive at a successful conclusion to his work.

11 Presentation

The way in which work is presented and displayed is extremely important. Badly presented work is always a disappointment. On the other hand, work which is well, and suitably, presented is shown to its maximum advantage.

There are two forms of presentation which most creative people will probably need to use at some time or other. One is the mounting of single items such as drawings, sketches, designs, etc, and the other is the layout, or arrangement, of several items on folio or display sheets for exhibition.

For mounting single two-dimensional items there are two basic approaches: mounting flat on to a background or cutting out a 'window' and fixing the work behind it.

The materials and tools needed are as follows:

Materials

For mounts: mounting card, available in various sizes, from art suppliers, in many colours and qualities.
For sticking: double- and single-sided clear adhesive tape (e.g. Sellotape); dry-mounting tissue, available from photographic suppliers; Cow Gum.

Tools

For cutting: guillotine; Stanley or Xacto knife with sharp blade; scissors, medium size, sharp.
For measuring and guiding: steel straight edge; ruler; set square; T-square.

Before mounting

After mounting

Tools and materials

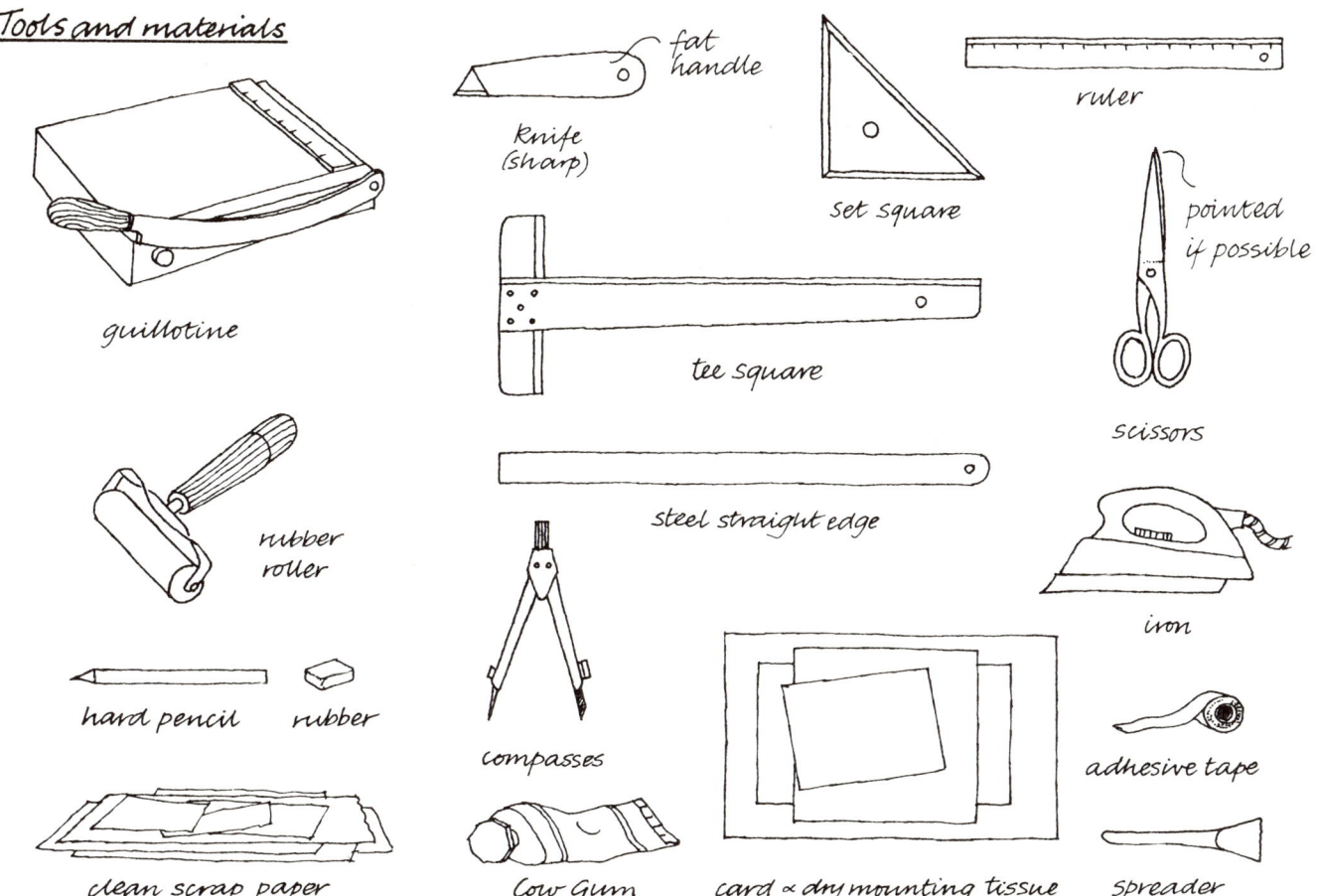

guillotine

knife (sharp) — fat handle

set square

ruler

tee square

scissors — pointed if possible

rubber roller

steel straight edge

iron

hard pencil

rubber

compasses

card & dry mounting tissue

adhesive tape

spreader

clean scrap paper

Cow Gum

For marking: hard pencil; pair of compasses or dividers.
For fixing and finishing: an iron; rubber roller (available from art suppliers and normally used for inking); rubber and clean paper.

Try always to keep your work clean — make sure hands are clean before starting. Some types of card need special care as they will absorb the natural oils from your hands and so tend to get shiny with handling.

Mounting flat on to a background:

Method
1 Mark out — in pencil — exactly where work needs to be trimmed. Corners should have 90° angles. Cut work to size using guillotine or straight edge and knife.
2 Select card for mount. Make sure it is larger than work (allowing for generous margins), and of a suitable colour.
3 Place work on mount so that the bottom margin is wider than the others. Move it about until it looks right.
4. Make pencil dots on the mount at the corners of the work. Check to see that these are parallel.
5 Place work back on mount, locating corner dots and draw round lightly with a hard pencil. The area inside this shape is for the adhesive.
6 Fixing (four alternatives)
Double-sided Sellotape. Fix in strips as shown, just *inside* pencil lines. Using both hands, position work over the strips and, when satisfied, lower gently from top downwards. When in place, cover with clean paper and press down firmly by hand.

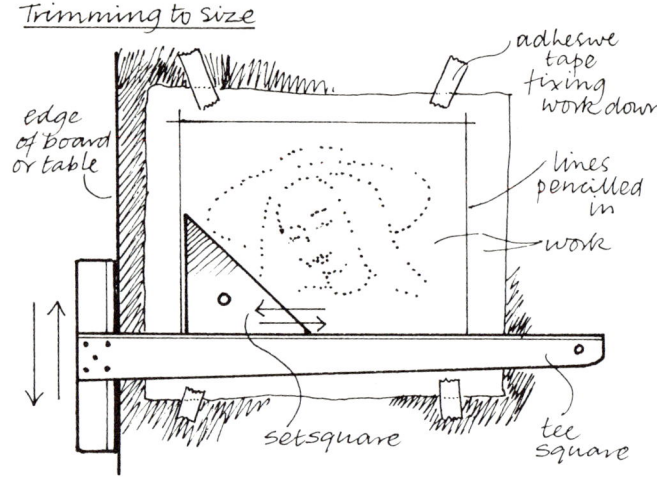

Trimming to size

adhesive tape fixing work down

edge of board or table

lines pencilled in work

setsquare

tee square

surplus cut away with guillotine or knife a straightedge

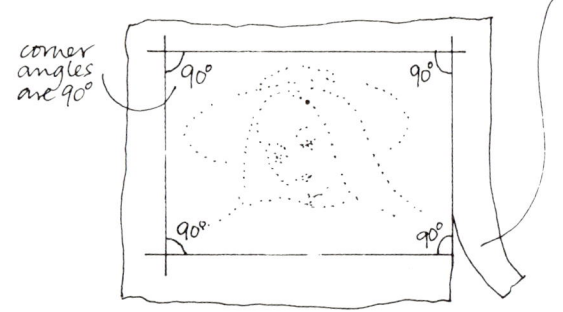

corner angles are 90°

90°   90°

90°   90°

Mounting flat on to a background

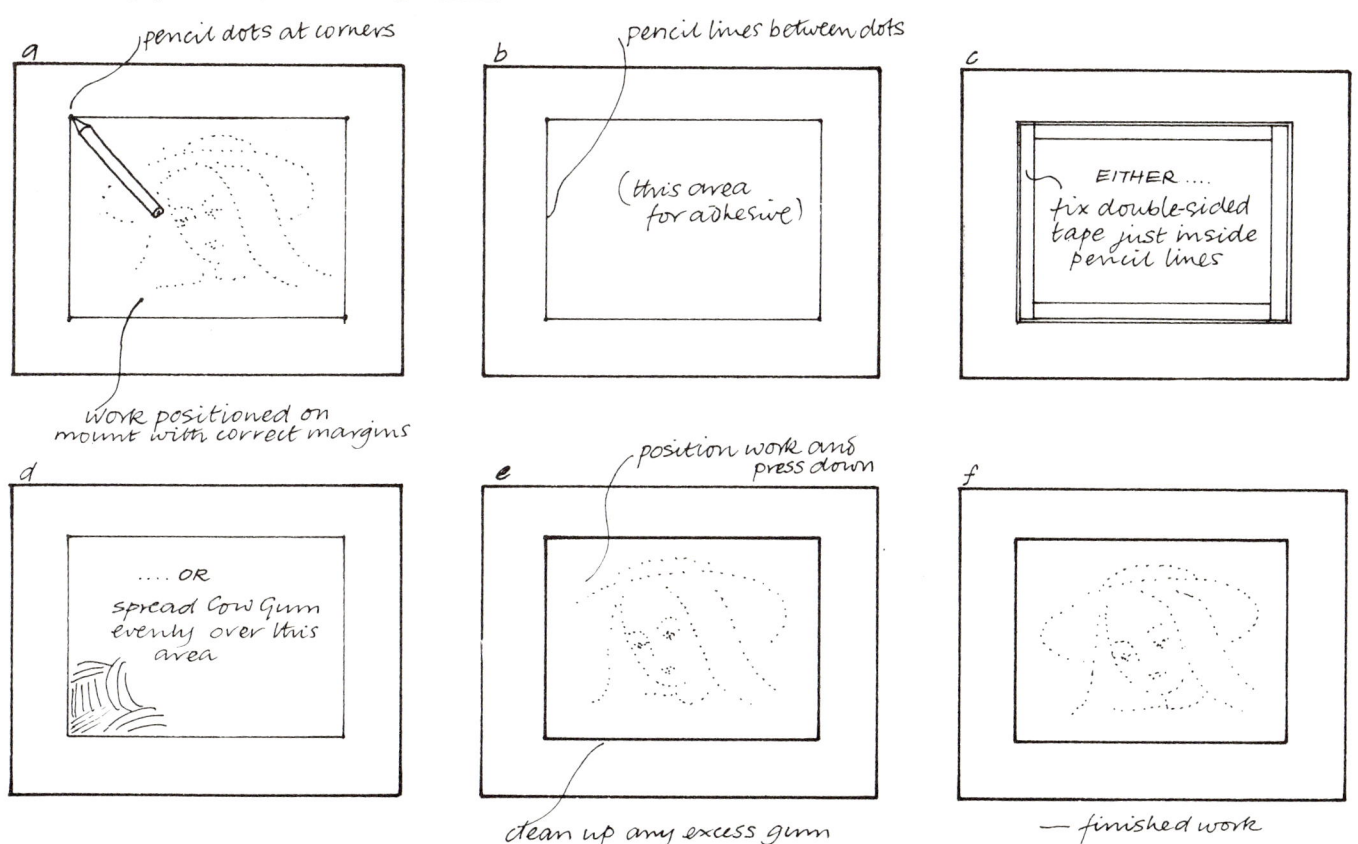

a — pencil dots at corners — work positioned on mount with correct margins

b — pencil lines between dots — (this area for adhesive)

c — EITHER.... fix double-sided tape just inside pencil lines

d — ....OR spread Cow Gum evenly over this area

e — position work and press down — clean up any excess gum

f — finished work

Cow Gum — single surface (see note on p. 100). Use spreader to make a thin even, film inside the pencil margins. Allow to dry for a few minutes until tacky. Position work over glued area and lower gently from top downwards. If a mistake is made in positioning carefully remove and re-position. Finally cover with a sheet of clean paper and press down firmly by hand or with rubber roller.

Cow Gum — double surface. Use spreader to make a thin, even, film on mount (inside pencil shape), and also coat back of work, going right up to the edges. When nearly dry, position and fix, using clean paper and roller to ensure that all edges are held firmly down. (It is very difficult to remove work, so positioning must be correct first time.)

Dry-mounting tissue. Used mainly for photographs, it has adhesive on both sides which needs *heat* to activate it. First let iron warm on a low heat. Place work face down and more than cover back with the tissue. Attach this in the centre and at each corner with the tip of the warm iron, as shown. Turn work over and trim neatly with scissors, or guillotine, to remove surplus tissue. Position on mount and cover with clean sheet of paper (thin). Iron *slowly* all over until the adhesive is stuck to both work and mount.

Some types of work do not take kindly to the heat of the iron so it is wise to experiment first before using this method of fixing.

Window mounting

Method
1   Trim work to correct size leaving a 1 cm margin all the way round. Draw in this margin, lightly, on the *back* of the work. Also draw a centre line as shown.

Using dry-mounting tissue

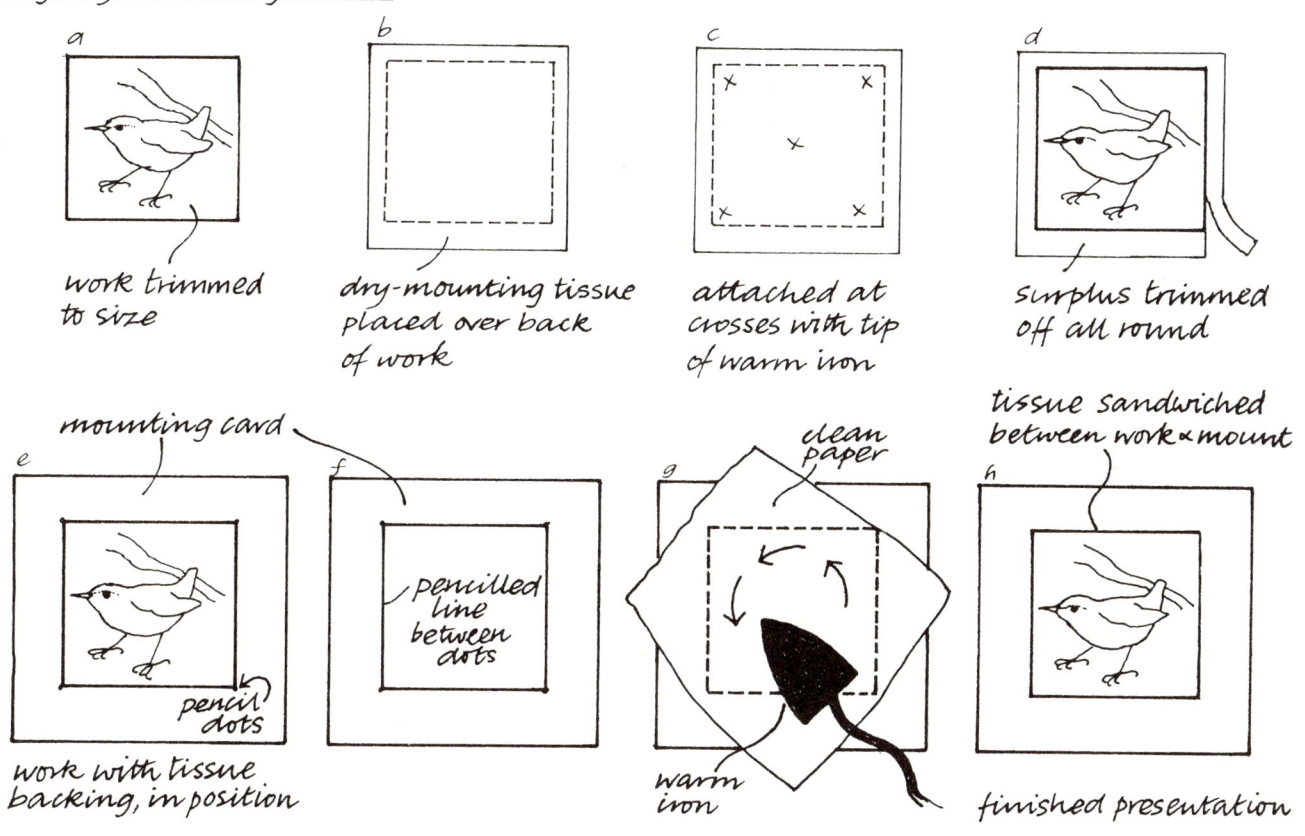

a work trimmed to size

b dry-mounting tissue placed over back of work

c attached at crosses with tip of warm iron

d surplus trimmed off all round

e mounting card / pencil dots / work with tissue backing, in position

f pencilled line between dots

g clean paper / warm iron

h tissue sandwiched between work & mount / finished presentation

Window mounting

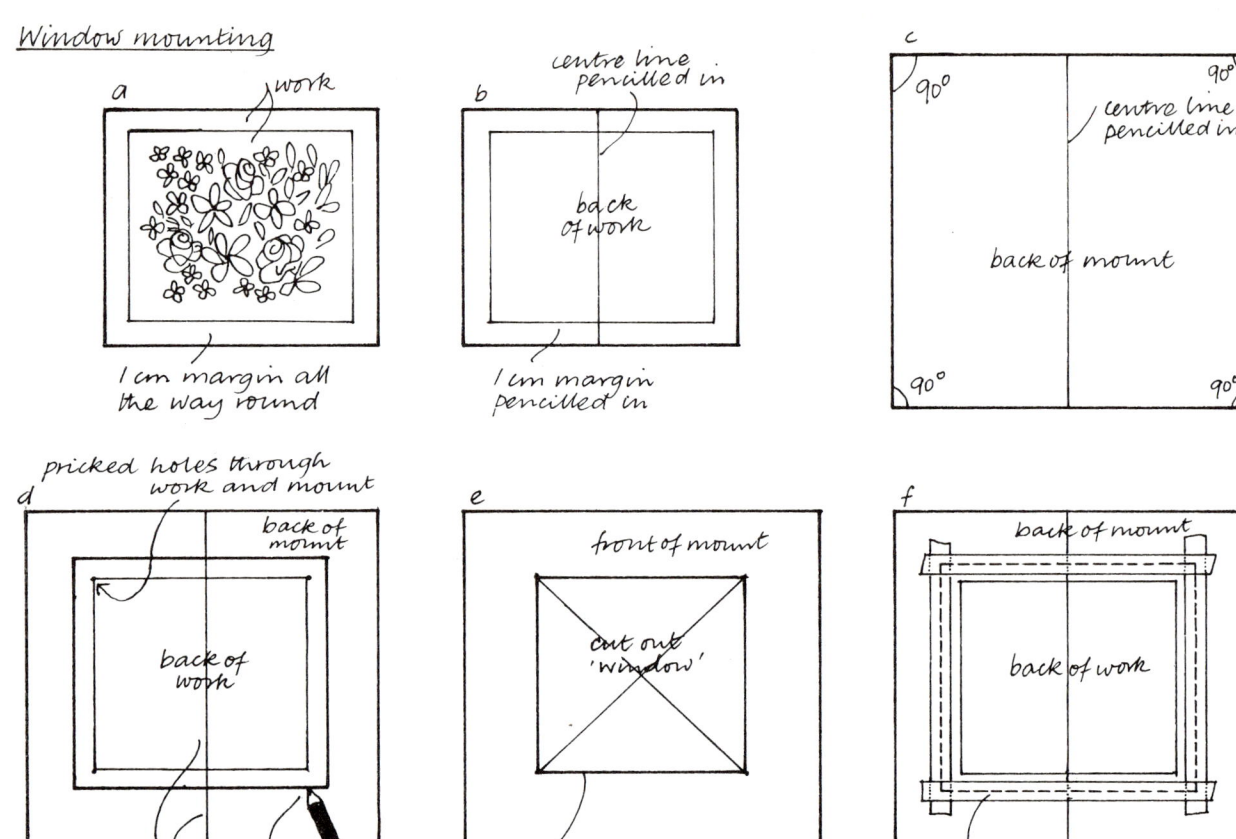

a work

1 cm margin all the way round

b centre line pencilled in

back of work

1 cm margin pencilled in

c 90°   90°

centre line pencilled in

back of mount

90°   90°

d pricked holes through work and mount

back of mount

back of work

lined up centres

work drawn round

e front of mount

cut out 'window'

pencil lines join up holes

f back of mount

back of work

adhesive tape

110

2 Select stiff card for mount, larger than work. Cut to size allowing generous margins, making sure its angles are 90°. On the *back* draw a centre line from top to bottom.

3 Move work about on mount until satisfied, matching up centre lines. Side margins should be equal and the bottom one slightly wider than the others. Draw round the outside of the work.

4 Take a pair of compasses or dividers and with a point prick pencilled corners *right through* to the front of the mounting card.

5 Turn mount over and work on the front. Using the four pricked holes pencil in the shape of the 'window'.

6 Using a metal straight edge and knife cut out the window. Be especially careful with the corners and make sure you cut cleanly through the card. A piece of waste card underneath to take the excess depth of cut will help. To make cutting easier the mount can be turned round.

7 Turn mount over and, using the pencil shape, position work (with the back towards you). Fix down neatly with tape as illustrated. Press down firmly by hand.

Layout of several items

An ordered arrangement of several items invites inspection. Haphazard layouts can look slovenly and baffling.

Grouping of items is an important feature of good layout; putting smaller things together to form a larger unit can avoid a spotty effect.

Generally speaking it is a mistake to put too much on one sheet. Two or three units are quite enough; however, too little on one sheet can be rather disconcerting.

Layout

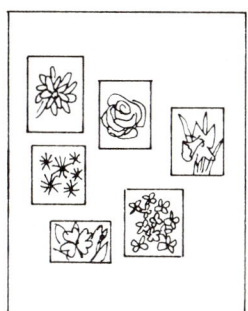

spotty effect of disordered units

small units closely grouped to form one unit

too many units give a 'plastered' effect

too few units give an empty feeling

111

When arranging several items on one sheet, look for any similarities in dimension that could be helpful. Are there any which could be made by cutting down the size of work, or grouping?

Implied lines and margins can be used as a basis for arrangements as shown. Heavy-toned items are usually best displayed at the bottom of layouts.

Items of work can either be mounted straight on to card, or window mounted. If too many windows are taken out the card may become weak. Always allow fairly generous margins and remember to increase the width of the bottom one.

Several sheets of mounted work may require careful planning and can be very successfully displayed if the layouts are *standardized*. For instance if there is a title on each one it can be positioned in the same place on each sheet. This gives a good sense of order and a feeling that the sheets are related.

Standardization of size of items is also very helpful (e.g. same-size outside margins, photographs, mounting sheets, labels, *wherever possible*).

If items of work differ a great deal in size and shape it may still be possible to use the same size mounting sheets and margins as shown.

Using the same *colour* mounting card can give a sense of order to several sheets but may not always be possible when showing a variety of work. A colour that suits one item may look wrong with another.

Presenting three-dimensional objects is a more complicated business and depends a great deal on the type of work involved. However, the same principles of grouping small items to form one unit still apply, as does the idea of standardization.

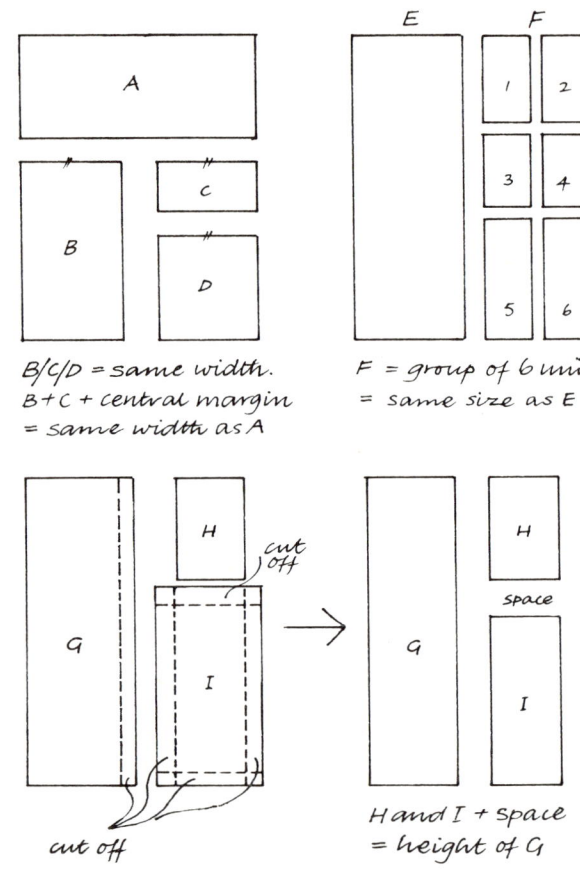

Similarities of measurement

B/C/D = same width.
B + C + central margin = same width as A

F = group of 6 units = same size as E

cut off

cut off

H and I + space = height of G

Standardisation – 4 layouts

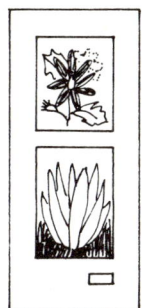  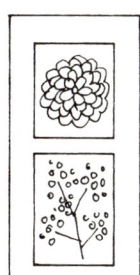 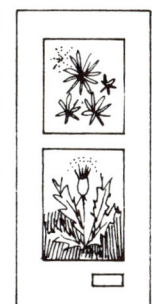

Standardisation

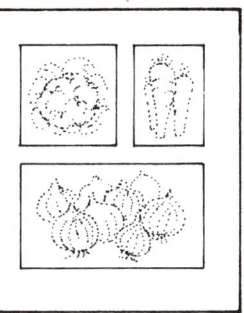 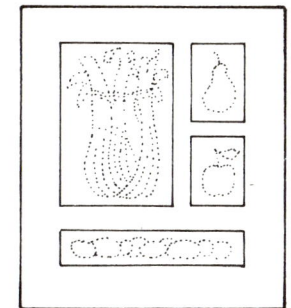

Size of mounts and outside margins are the same in each example

Tone arrangement

top heavy layout

heavy tone looks better lower down

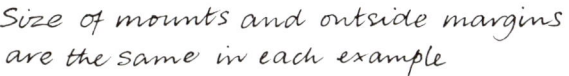

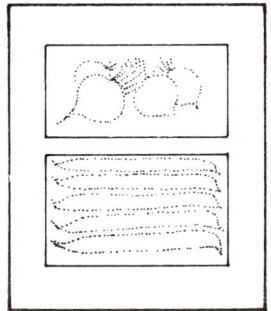 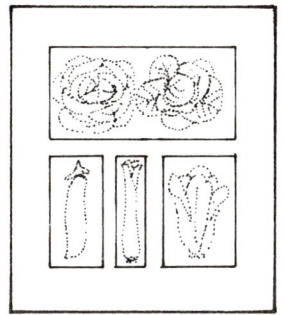

Although units vary in size and shape a sense of order is accomplished

Again, too many items in one arrangement are unsatisfactory and can look like a jumble sale. Unless very precious or large, one item on its own can look rather lonely.

Visually heavy items look best at the bottom of vertical arrangements, as shown.

Labelling for all kinds of work can also be standardized. Handwritten labels, unless professionally lettered, can look very disappointing. There are several kinds of 'instant' lettering available which will stick to card and paper, but these too, unless handled well, will look amateurish. Neatly-typed labels can look good if cleanly trimmed. The word content of labels should always be kept to a minimum.

Presentation is very much a question of personal style as well as technique. The small details such as neat corners, cleanliness and quality of mounting materials can be as important as the actual layout. It represents an *attitude of mind* that can improve or mar work accordingly. Time and trouble taken in presenting work is rarely wasted, as an ordered, thoughtful arrangement will generally encourage attention and interest.

Display

too many items can give
a 'jumble sale' effect

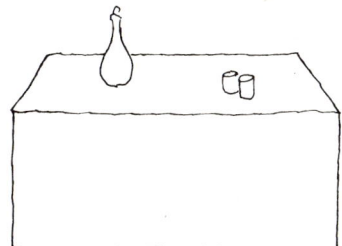

too few items look lonely
unless very special or
very large

too many items the same
height look very dull

Standardisation

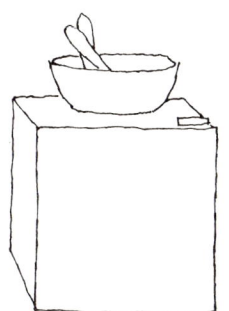

Same size stands, labels in similar position on each

heaviest items look best
at the bottom of display

115

12 Artists and craftsmen

It is remarkable that so many hundreds of thousands of people want to be artists, for only a very small number are successful in making a living. Usually they have to take on another occupation, such as teaching, in order to survive.

Training as an artist usually takes the form of several years at a school or college. It begins with an experimental period leading to specialization in one or more subjects.

Artists usually try to sell their work privately or through small galleries, mainly in London and other major cities. Local museums and municipal galleries encourage new talent where possible. To promote artists' work *exhibitions* are held. These are either mixed exhibitions where a number of artists show their work or a one-man show which is exclusively for one artist.

Very occasionally society produces an artist who is prepared to work out on a limb, not within the confines of an artistic movement. This type of artist, although an outsider, often has great value as his work will be entirely original and of a very personal nature. Only the most dedicated artist can survive in this context.

Designers train in a similar way to artists and can work either for a firm, or freelance. Clients are found privately or by an agency.

The craftsman is usually trained actually at work with a master-craftsman under the apprenticeship system. He can hope to make a steady, if modest, living provided there is sufficient demand for his craft.

The charts show how artists and craftsmen function in relation to society and how their roles differ.

116

Possible influences on work

wealth
materials
opportunity

work of others
environment
tradition

culture
climate

artists   craftsmen

health
physique
age

intelligence
experience
personality

energy
imagination
education

motive
nationality

Artists and craftsmen – how they function

Artist – concerned with expressing ideas and feelings

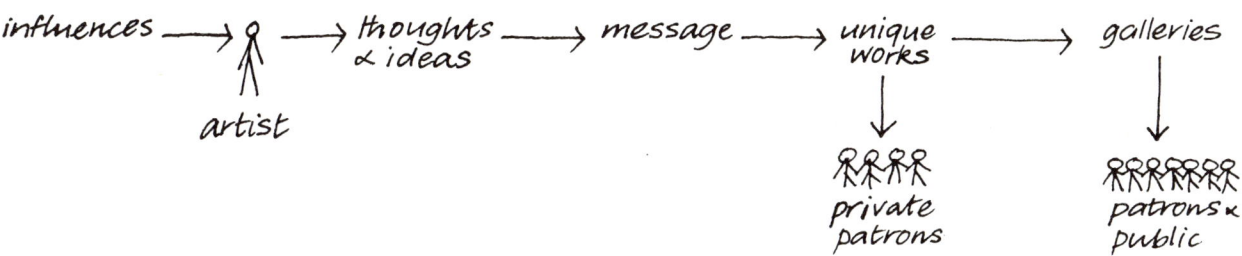

influences → artist → thoughts & ideas → message → unique works → galleries

unique works → private patrons

galleries → patrons & public

Craftsman – focuses on skill and the way things are made

influences + demand & basic idea → craftsman → application of skill → products (variations on basic idea) → shops

products → public

shops → public

Artists/craftsmen/designers - how they function

Artist/craftsman - concentrates on expressing ideas → products skilfully made

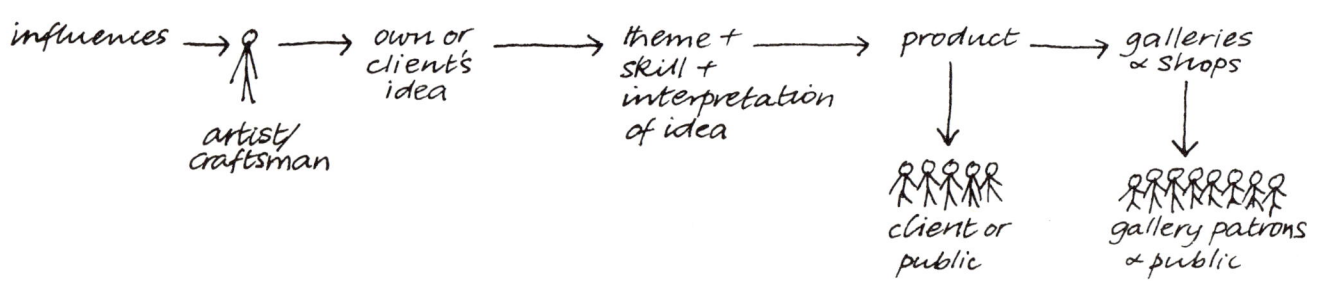

Designer - concerned with ideas and their interpretation for industry

influences → designer → ideas → designs → technical interpretation → mass production of goods by manufacturer → shops

↓ wholesalers

↓ public

Art Movement

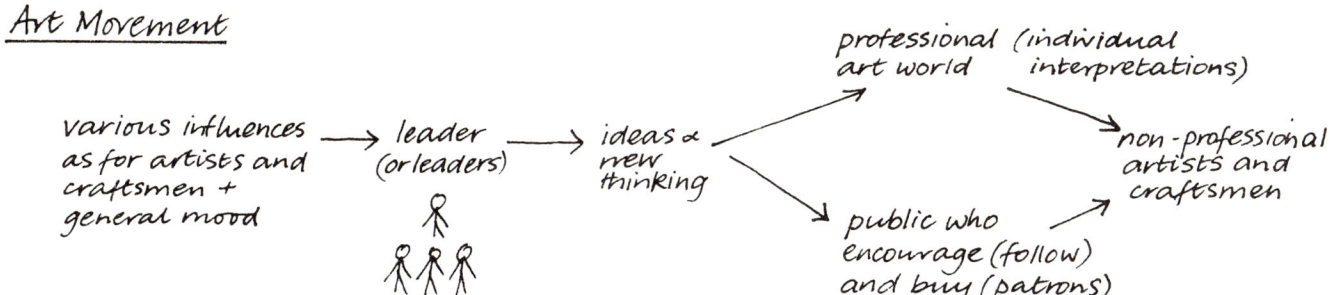

various influences
as for artists and
craftsmen +
general mood → leader
(or leaders) → ideas &
new
thinking → professional (individual
art world   interpretations)

→ non-professional
artists and
craftsmen

→ public who
encourage (follow)
and buy (patrons)

Fashion Movement

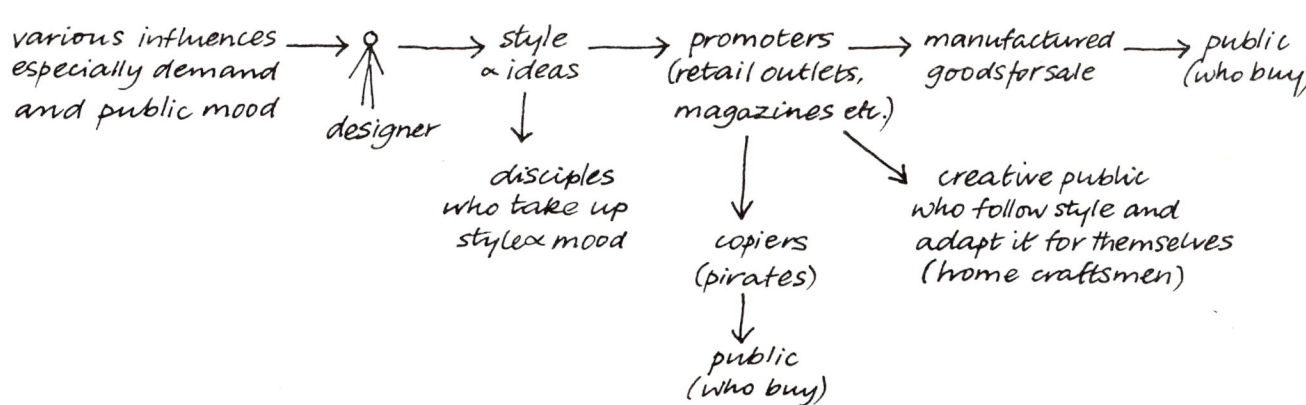

various influences
especially demand
and public mood → designer → style
& ideas → promoters
(retail outlets,
magazines etc.) → manufactured
goods for sale → public
(who buy)

↓
disciples
who take up
style & mood

↓
copiers
(pirates)

↓
public
(who buy)

→ creative public
who follow style and
adapt it for themselves
(home craftsmen)

The amateur artist or craftsman has an important role to play in keeping alive arts and crafts which are in danger of dying out. Libraries, education centres and craft societies provide instruction and encouragement for those who wish to spend their leisure time creatively. Enviably, the amateur can work with the best motive of all — that of creating art for the love of it.

13 Exercises

Colour and tone

1 Using the three primaries, make a colour chart of the same sort as that in chapter two. Match the colours as carefully as you can.

2 By mixing the three primaries make the nearest possible colour to black.

3 Take one hue, yellow, and gradually add portions of white to give you a range of tints. Using the same basic yellow add portions of its complementary colour (violet) to give you a range of shades.

4 Using black and white, copy the tone chart from Chapter 1. Mix other colours from the three primaries and try to estimate their tone value.

5 Cut out small portions of colour from magazines and arrange them in groups to make colour schemes – monochromatic, polychromatic and analogous.

6 Study the work of one artist, in reproduction or in the original and note his colour preferences. What colour does he use most?

Texture and pattern

1 Collect small scraps of paper, fabric, etc., all of one colour, and arrange on a sheet of paper.

2 Collect all kinds of things which are textured – leaves, bark, fabric (any colour). Arrange them in a scale ranging from smooth to coarse.

3 Make rubbings of various textures, using a black wax crayon and kitchen paper. Cut them into rectangles and squares and make a collage.

4 Take some pieces of wallpaper and printed fabric and try to work out the 'units of repeat' in the patterns printed on them.

Shape and form

1 On two large sheets of paper, or in two exercise books if more convenient, stick cut-out photographs or pictures of shapes and forms, (a) that appeal to you and (b) that you find unattractive.

2 Study in detail the work of one sculptor and one painter that appeals to you. Read as much as you can of their backgrounds to help you understand their work.

3 Study such natural forms as you might find illustrated in books on geography, geology and natural history, e.g. rock formations, crystals, etc.

Style and function

1 Study the Art Nouveau period, especially its background. A useful springboard is *Art Nouveau* by Martin Battersby, published by Hamlyn in paperback (1970).

2 Describe the function of each piece of a set of cutlery, and note how they are designed. Could any of them be improved in your view?

3 Try to design a simple functional article.

4 Study natural objects such as shells, honeycomb, and seed pods and relate their forms to their function.

121

Composition

1 Make several *collages* (arrangements) with magazine cuttings, scraps of fabric, etc., cutting the pieces up and moving them around until you are satisfied. Finally stick them on to sheets of thin card or paper.
2 Arrange a still-life of kitchen ware — crockery, pots and pans, etc. — moving the items about, adding and subtracting items until you think the group looks right.
3 Analyse other people's compositions — paintings, advertising material, etc.

General

1 Take up a craft as a hobby.
2 Visit your local library and regularly browse through the art reference section.
3 *Read* art books.
4 Visit exhibitions and museums whenever you can, especially if you go abroad for holidays. Do not try to take in too much at one visit. It is better to confine your interest to one or two sections at a time.
5 Find out what your local education authority has to offer in the way of art-appreciation classes, practical craft instruction, educational trips, etc.
6 Read the art columns in the newspapers and periodicals to find out what is going on in the art world.
7 If you get the opportunity, talk to artists about *their* work.
8 Make a habit of supporting your local art community whenever possible, visiting local exhibitions, etc.
9 Make time in your life for creative expression so that it becomes an important part of your life. It should more than reward you, and others.

Size and proportion

1 Make as many measurements and comparisons as possible from your own body. Can you find any relationships?
2 To help you understand the application of the Golden Section, study the work of the Ancient Greeks, particularly their architecture, e.g. the Parthenon.

Illusion and perspective

1 Try to find examples of optical illusions.
2 Copy all the perspective drawings from this book, freehand.
3 Study paintings which include architecture and try to understand the artist's use of perspective.
4 Look at some landscape paintings and discover the horizon (eye level) in each if you can.
5 Search through magazines and find photographs with unusually high or low eye levels.

Drawing and sketching

1 Try out various media and papers.
2 Copy a drawing by someone else.
3 Study the drawings of one particular artist.
4 Make a sight-size drawing or sketch.
5 Keep a sketch book and use it every day for a few minutes to sketch the world around you.